Robert,

   An early copy of this book for a man I greatly admire... Thank you for allowing me to work alongside of you to transform healthcare in our community and create an example for the industry!

   To Health Optimization!

   Jeff

NOT
JUST
IN
SICKNESS
BUT
ALSO IN
HEALTH

JEFF MARGOLIS

NOT JUST IN SICKNESS,
BUT ALSO IN HEALTH

MOVING BEYOND SICKCARE TO HEALTH OPTIMIZATION FOR ALL

ForbesBooks

Published by ForbesBooks, Charleston, South Carolina.
Member of Advantage Media Group.

ForbesBooks is a registered trademark, and the ForbesBooks colophon is a trademark of Forbes Media, LLC.

Printed in the United States of America.

10 9 8 7 6 5 4 3 2 1

ISBN: 978-1-94663-389-7
LCCN: 2020918100

Cover design by David Taylor.
Layout design by Wesley Strickland.

This custom publication is intended to provide accurate information and the opinions of the author in regard to the subject matter covered. It is sold with the understanding that the publisher, Advantage|ForbesBooks, is not engaged in rendering legal, financial, or professional services of any kind. If legal advice or other expert assistance is required, the reader is advised to seek the services of a competent professional.

 Advantage Media Group is proud to be a part of the Tree Neutral® program. Tree Neutral offsets the number of trees consumed in the production and printing of this book by taking proactive steps such as planting trees in direct proportion to the number of trees used to print books. To learn more about Tree Neutral, please visit **www.treeneutral.com**.

Since 1917, Forbes has remained steadfast in its mission to serve as the defining voice of entrepreneurial capitalism. ForbesBooks, launched in 2016 through a partnership with Advantage Media Group, furthers that aim by helping business and thought leaders bring their stories, passion, and knowledge to the forefront in custom books. Opinions expressed by ForbesBooks authors are their own. To be considered for publication, please visit **www.forbesbooks.com**.

*This book is dedicated to the memory of
my friend and industry colleague, Thomas J. Main (1955–2018).
Tom was a great and humble human being and a healthcare strategy
consulting genius. If Tom were still with us in person (he is certainly
with us in spirit) he would affirm the importance of this book
and tell me how to improve it. I'm listening!*

I ... take thee ... in sickness and in health; for richer,

for poorer; to love and to cherish; for better, for worse;

from this day forward; till death do us part.

—excerpts from a traditional wedding vow

CONTENTS

FORMING A LASTING UNION BETWEEN YOU AND YOUR HEALTH

In a world where attention spans seem to be getting shorter, headlines dominate 24-7 news cycles and social feeds, and the written word is increasingly replaced with hieroglyphic-like emojis, it may seem futile to write a book. I am reluctantly resigned to the fact that comprehensive long-form thinking has given way to sound bites. As the chairman and formative past CEO of Welltok, the leading enterprise consumer activation company in healthcare, and before that the founder, chairman, and CEO of TriZetto, even my primary occupation of developing data and software-driven solutions to complex problems operates in an environment where snippets of code are produced in short sprints. The truth is, there is a relatively small percentage of the population that relishes solving a difficult problem end to end. And what problem looms larger in the United States than affordable, effective healthcare for an extraordinarily diverse society?

Even among those who can solve demanding problems, a still smaller percentage have the energy and will to document the solution adequately so that others can benefit from understanding the underpinnings of and pathway to it. This book is a sincere and passionate effort to communicate sufficiently, without excessive embellishment, how we will achieve the next major breakthrough in advancing the value of a healthcare system that has heretofore excluded the most important actor in the equation—the consumer. Unfortunately, my message cannot be communicated without a progression of concepts that will help those endeavoring to fix healthcare apply sound principles. Perhaps, then, it is natural that throughout my career as a healthcare information technology leader, I have been told my affinity for teaching is a central part of my leadership style.

In my value system, the greatest respect you can show others is to listen to and learn from what they say, to patiently but convincingly teach them what you think you know that can help them be successful, and to rejoice when a team of people comes together and does both in abundance. At the risk of sounding clichéd, I often refer to a quotation that was on the wall of the jazz band practice room at the University of Illinois in Champaign, where I attended college. My recollection is that it said, "To be truly innovative, you must first be steeped in tradition." It is a lesson that I have taken to heart throughout my life. To me, it means that you must take the time and demonstrate the discipline to learn what others already know about a subject before you claim improvisational prowess. In other words, in the overused vernacular of business today, you had best understand what is going on if you hope to *disrupt or transform* something. But I must admit I am a bit confused when I consider that even as the body of knowledge rapidly increases in nearly every subject known to humankind, the rigor that is applied to cementing that body of knowledge in the minds of students and professionals seems to be diminishing.

Today we produce specialists who were never generalists. This naturally creates siloed behaviors. We have the great majority of investment capital in society "managed" and distributed by people who have minimally or perhaps never operated a business or professional enterprise. Higher education without "in the trenches" experience makes it difficult to distinguish important and real innovation from ethereal valuations based on spreadsheet models. And in the past decade or so, we began defining a demigod class system of people called software "engineers" and data "scientists." But as with athletes, the truly great ones are rare. Similarly, advances in data storage, processing

Higher education without "in the trenches" experience makes it difficult to distinguish important and real innovation from ethereal valuations based on spreadsheet models.

speed, and transfer rates have allowed economists, statisticians, mathematicians, social scientists, physical scientists, and environmental scientists to produce quantitative models that crunch yottabytes of data. But in most cases the data scientists cannot produce accurate multivariate predictions. Of course, even a broken clock is right twice a day, and occasionally fame is earned for a great predictive call—some might call it luck. But accurate predictions are rarely repeated by the same person or team even twice. This is why I like accountants. They do arithmetic exceedingly well, apply consistent rules across a systematic set of variables, and produce answers that are amazingly accurate. And because they have a method to discern what is true and tend to be fact-based, accountants are surprisingly interesting and pleasant at cocktail parties.

Ensuring prerequisite knowledge to foster breakthrough innovation is why I wrote my prior book, *The Healthcare Cure* (Prometheus, 2011). It was intended to support people who want to advance or successfully navigate the healthcare industry by creating a useful framework of understanding for people trying to figure out the moving parts of the US healthcare system. My professional career initially developed in the information systems consulting business, so I was exposed to methods of applying systems science and information technology to solve complex problems in energy, mining, banking, manufacturing and distribution, pharmaceuticals, and healthcare delivery. Eventually I chose to focus my efforts entirely in the healthcare sector. Building from the expertise I developed over the course of two decades, the primary focus of *The Healthcare Cure* was conveyed by its subtitle: "How Sharing Information Can Make the System Work Better." Because the book was steeped in tradition and generalized knowledge, its systematic teachings have held up exceedingly well over the past decade. This is probably due much less to any prescience on my part than it is to the opportunities I have had to experience Malcom Gladwell's ten-thousand-hour rule across the multiple subjects of healthcare, information technology, accounting and finance, management and entrepreneurship, and leadership. I continue to seek to learn every day. And one thing I keep learning—and I want to say this politely—is that there is a tendency in some of the smartest people I know to assume that their intelligence alone, without regard for the as-is environment and a deep understanding of how it came to be, will drive breakthrough thinking.

The reality is that we need breakthrough thinking if we hope to solve the complex conundrums that form the various sectors making up what we refer to as the healthcare system, but we cannot divorce our solutions, no matter how visionary, from the system as it exists, however ailing it might be. My hope is that naming this book as a catchy sound bite, *Not Just in Sickness ... But Also in Health*, will intrigue readers to delve a bit deeper than usual into the irony of the suboptimal healthcare system we've come to expect and accept, a system that produces insufficient value—too little quality for too much cost. It focuses on episodic and chronic care, when what we really need is a system that desires to achieve optimal health for all individuals. We need a system that operates out of a recognition that true optimal health and total well-being include the whole of a person and not only the traditional medical metrics. Such an approach can also eliminate avoidable inequities that plague our population. To be clear, the objective is not to attack or criticize incumbent industry actors. The incumbent entities all developed for sound reasons at various points in time. Rather, there is an important and vital opportunity for every player in both the as-is and the to-be worlds of healthcare to optimize health for all by adding some harmonies and countermelodies to the traditional tune of healthcare that will create a far more complete and balanced composition.

Part I: In Sickness *and* in Health

From Sickcare to Health Optimization

CHAPTER 1

WHAT IF THE HEALTHCARE SYSTEM WAS DESIGNED TO MAKE PEOPLE HEALTHIER AT A LOWER COST?

It is absolutely possible to substantially improve the health and total well-being of individuals comprising any population—including our nation—while reducing total spend. And while doing so will require some systematic changes to how the healthcare industry operates in the United States today, the road to achieve this is neither radical nor frightening. In fact, nearly every seasoned healthcare industry leader and policy influencer—and I interact with many— already understands that the approach I am explaining is required. Fortunately, this is one of those rare cases where people with diverse backgrounds can readily agree on the "what" once they see it put into understandable terms. Unfortunately, understanding the "how" in terms of making it actionable and real has, thus far, broadly eluded both highly experienced healthcare professionals and individuals who just want to have better health at a lower cost. Let's explore how we can transform the healthcare system to deliver far more value than it does today and continuously improve that value over time.

Today Healthcare Is Mostly Sickcare

Even if you have a chronic health condition, like I do—I was diagnosed with Crohn's disease at age nineteen—or you have suffered a significant acute health event, the reality is that you will likely spend less than 1 percent of your life in clinical settings or clinical interactions. Yet what do you picture in your mind when you think of healthcare? Your doctor's office? The hospital? Not only do most of us think of healthcare in terms of physician's offices, urgent care centers, hospitals, and pharmacies, but we have also become accustomed to a healthcare system that doesn't pay a lot of attention to the other 99 percent of our time. Of course, each of us lives in differing patterns from one another. How I spend my time is likely a great deal different than how you spend yours, just as my health needs and my lifestyle patterns are certainly different than yours. Our current healthcare system, one that I long ago termed the *sickcare* system, focuses almost entirely on the 1 percent and fundamentally ignores the 99 percent. And to be clear, this limited 1 percent time we spend in clinical settings and interactions includes current trends like telemedicine visits and homecare visits. But such care delivery methods, whether in person or virtual, generally share a central theme of the sickcare approach—*they exist to fix or treat what ails patients*. Because of this mindset, the entrenched sickcare system allocates much of its focus to providing access to services for the costliest and neediest of our population. And let's acknowledge that the coronavirus pandemic of 2020 exemplified how sickcare thinking dominated our culture, as a new disease threat drowned out long-established vital and important clinical services—and altered patterns in daily living—that negatively impacted far more people than COVID-19.

The sickcare system is primarily *reactive*. Traditional clinical care was developed to provision and allocate scarce human and technological resources (e.g., doctors and medicines) for when we need care that we cannot provide for ourselves. In doing so, it is a system that, in failing to understand and impact the other 99 percent of our time, also fails to adequately provision solutions to assist us in our everyday living behaviors and choices. Yet—and this is key—it is the behaviors and choices we make nearly every day of our lives that drive 70 percent of our health and well-being status. In fact, while I use the 70 percent mark as the percentage of our total health that is driven by everyday living, many researchers suggest that traditional medical care only accounts for 10 to 20 percent of the modifiable contributors to healthy outcomes for a population.[1] At 70 percent, I am being conservative regarding the role that daily living and social determinant factors (health-related behaviors, socioeconomic factors, and environmental factors) play in our total health.

What Drives Health Status?

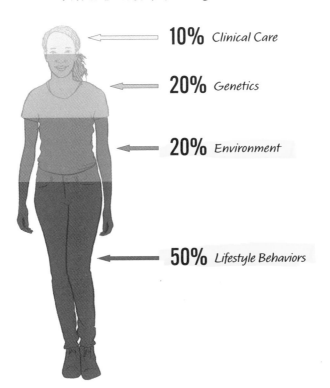

10% *Clinical Care*

20% *Genetics*

20% *Environment*

50% *Lifestyle Behaviors*

Because it largely ignores this 70 percent of factors that drive our health status, the sickcare system dedicates nearly all its resources and a substantial majority of its costs to a small proportion of the total population. The result is what is referred to in the healthcare industry as the upside-down pyramid. Data generated by the healthcare industry reveal that about 15 percent of the population produces between 65 and 80 percent of the cost:[2]

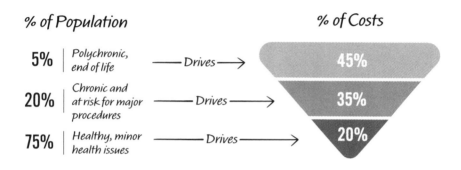

Driving Better Healthcare Value Requires Expanded Thinking

What are the full implications of whom the current sickcare system serves most often today, and what does this mean to total population health and cost? In my 2011 book, *The Healthcare Cure*, I introduced a simple equation that is central to understanding the cost and value challenge in the way the healthcare system works:

$$\text{Healthcare Value} = \frac{\textit{Health Status (person or population)}}{\textit{Total Cost of Care}}$$

The equation was put forth to quantify the idea that if we are to achieve better value in the healthcare system, then we must drive better health status (i.e., outcomes) for every dollar spent. Let's move this equation forward into today's world and see if we can use it to inform a better tomorrow.

If you'll allow me to abbreviate the concept of healthcare value as "H_v" and apply what we've discussed so far, another way to express this same equation in our traditional sickcare system is as follows:

$$H_v = \frac{\textit{Health Status (person or population)}}{\textit{Sickcare (docs + hospitals + Rx + Dx + med equipment + supplies)}}$$

I realize not everybody likes math, but this equation simply says that we achieve higher value if the health of a person or population is good (e.g., normal blood pressure) while costs are lower (e.g., fewer doctor visits, fewer expensive drugs, and avoidance of hospital stays). The current healthcare system was developed to provision access to the items in the denominator because most of us do not hold licenses to diagnose, treat, or prescribe medical care. The current system was also designed to establish limits or controls for utilizing these resources because they are, in simple terms, relatively expensive. As a natural consequence, our society endlessly debates the cost of and access to the sickcare components. It is this topic that led to the concept and development of what we call managed care. It's a useful debate in some ways, but it won't solve the healthcare affordability crisis because this equation is incomplete when you just plug the traditional sickcare components into the denominator, as I did above. Remember, these familiar clinical cost components generally drive less than 30 percent of health status, and we utilize them less than 1 percent of the time.

Bear with me as we advance the equation to be more holistic. Consider the following more generalized language:

$$H_v = \frac{\textit{Health Status (person or population)}}{\textit{Inputs to Health}}$$

This hopefully seems like common sense. Why would anybody choose to do something more complicated and expensive regarding their health if they can achieve the same outcome more easily and at a lower cost? This does beg the question of what the "inputs to health" are. For now, as we've discussed, let's just say that those inputs are far more than sickcare. Because some, if not many, would regard sickcare as a pejorative term, let's substitute the more encompassing description "clinical care," and now let's add room into the equation for those things we do that drive 70 percent of our health and where we spend over 99 percent of our time. Let's call those things "daily living." And, so as not to prolong your agony, let's recast the denominator in the same equation as the following:

$$H_v = \frac{\textit{Health Status (person or population)}}{\textit{Clinical Care + Daily Living}}$$

The concept of "daily living" is just as it sounds. What do you do every day? You eat, sleep, work, walk, drive, watch media, and socialize. In other words, you undertake a series of actions as you go about the 99 percent of your life. Many of these actions impact your health status, and almost all of them affect your "total well-being"—but more on that later.

We developed managed care in the United States to put systematic organizing principles around the resources and cost components for the first category of the denominator—clinical care. I personally spent over twenty years of my career building organizations and sophisticated information technology solutions to do just that. Honestly, we're pretty good at traditional managed care, although there is room for improvement. But even if we were to perfect it, we already know that we would be perfecting those things that drive 30 percent of our health.

What if by systematically focusing on the *daily living* activities of individuals, which impact 70 percent of our health, we could simultaneously drive more efficient usage of scarce and expensive sickcare resources that impact the other 30 percent? What if we were able to systematically apply the power of modern data and information technology to provision health improvement resources for *daily living*, personalized to each individual? What if we helped everyone connect to a combination of the clinical and daily living resources they need to achieve and sustain

> *Achieving and sustaining the highest health status at the lowest cost is the definition of "health optimization."*

their best health status at the lowest cost? Achieving and sustaining the highest health status at the lowest cost is the definition of "health optimization" that is used throughout this book.

Individual People/Diverse Needs

If we really want to make people and populations healthier at lower total cost, we first must recognize that health optimization is not a one-size-fits-all problem to be solved. That being said, a common systematic approach is necessary to drive personalization at scale across millions or billions of people. Amazon long ago figured out that each of us will fill our "shopping carts" differently based on our interests, our lifestyles, and our needs. But the brick-and-mortar stores that predated Amazon already knew that. In other words, Amazon's digital innovation was steeped in analog tradition. But amid the many challenges faced by the healthcare industry, it has not yet figured out how to organize the inventory of things that impact 70 percent of our health into a commonly categorized and repeatable system.

Think of it this way: Unlike your local grocery store, the online shopping experience of Amazon, or even the chain convenience store on the corner, the healthcare industry doesn't know how to sort all of its products and services into shopping aisles. Instead it has traditionally segmented us into sickcare cohorts based upon our clinically diagnosed diseases, or lack thereof. This has been done for the benefit of healthcare providers and health insurers so they can allocate their scarce resources in a way that they understand and attempt to rein in the costs of expensive services, medicines, and supplies. As a result, we live in a world of segmented labels: "He's type 2 diabetic," "She's pregnant," "They're obese and hypertensive."

The healthcare industry has spent the better part of the past thirty years getting the clinical care inputs into categories that can be priced and managed. But we have barely begun to classify and categorize health improvement resources that could be applied to daily living into something that is comprehensible for industry players such as health plans, providers, and employers, much less individual consumers like you and me. Since our daily living is diverse and our needs vary according to our individual situation, the health improvement resources that must be lined up for each of us to achieve optimal health must be varied in a personalized way as well.

Let's humanize these concepts by considering four individuals that we will reference throughout this book. These illustrations are central to conveying how healthcare needs, health insurance benefits, and daily living social determinants inexorably meld together in real life. In other words, let's view people as people and not as cohorts of those with traditional sickcare labels.

Sarah

Sarah is a low-income, young, single mother living in an impoverished urban community. She works evenings and some nights at a wage that places her family near the poverty level, but her job status does not afford her health insurance. She is reliant on low-cost public transportation, which is not always safe when she uses it. Friends and relatives help with childcare when they are able, but their scheduling is unreliable, and many of these informal helpers face their own problems with poor health, poverty, and substance dependency. She is trying to make ends meet while maintaining her own personal dignity and derives her health benefits through a state Medicaid program. She attempts to manage her type 2 diabetes but does so irregularly and does not easily have access to affordable food that can aid her condition. One of her children is asthmatic. There is a mix of private, largely nonprofit support service programs, including religious and other charitable resources alongside county and local public agencies, available in her community. These resources are difficult to navigate or access, and she has only peripheral awareness of their offerings. If she can put such resources to use, she theoretically has access to health counseling, pregnancy care, immunization programs, and the like. But she has little guidance about how to best use them. Piecing these services together can be the difference between finding a path to at least a modicum of health, well-being, and success and being in a position where she can repeatedly end up in desperate, overdue need of sickcare services. Her life feels like a constant, narrow, and shaky balance beam.

Fred

Fred is a seventy-five-year-old Medicare recipient whose body is becoming increasingly frail. He has no significant chronic conditions but is becoming susceptible to falls and anything that might compromise his naturally weakening immune system. Despite relatively good health, Fred's blood sugar level classifies him as prediabetic, his blood pressure is on the high end of the acceptable range, and he has developed minor cardiovascular disease as age is taking its toll. His wife has been recently diagnosed with Alzheimer's after enduring a multiyear battle with breast cancer. After a lifetime of relying on the normal social and positive relationship support of his wife, extended family, and friends, Fred's circumstances are shifting. Suddenly the person who has been his life partner is fading in physical and behavioral health, and he must now help provide care and support for his wife. Many of his friends are passing away or moving into advanced care environments. His grown children are geographically scattered, with families of their own. He has Medicare health benefits, and he and his wife live in an independent living senior community, so there is a support system around him. Nonetheless, he encounters a plethora of challenges to knowing how best to maintain his own health and manage their economics. He is not poor, but he is not wealthy enough to afford full-time assistance for his wife, and he constantly wonders if her needs are reaching a level beyond his abilities. He purposefully wants to be able to pass some economic wealth to his children, despite the fact that some of them do not regularly provide him even a conversational relationship or other support. As a result, he underspends on himself, living a life only focused on day-to-day necessities. Fred feels increasingly isolated and lonely, ever aware that his independence is slipping away as he "rounds third base," but he wants to be responsible and finish strong

María

María is a middle-class married mother of two with a daughter who is in her junior year of college and a son who graduated from college two years ago. She had her first child at twenty-nine. Her marriage is solid. Both she and her husband work. They have a bit of money saved and put away in retirement accounts. She has the support of the classic commercial healthcare system, with a high-deductible PPO insurance plan provided through her employer, although her out-of-pocket costs seems to increase annually and take a larger and larger percentage of their household economic pie. Of the couple's parents, one is deceased, and two of the three remaining have significant health issues, with María's recently widowed mother living in financially precarious circumstances. María and her husband still owe a substantial sum on their mortgage, and their children are accumulating student loan debt, which María hopes to help pay off. Between paying for their children's college education and assisting María's mother, the family's savings are being drained. Normal middle-age health concerns are setting in with creeping weight gain and reduction in physical fitness. María is the quintessential household decision maker on healthcare issues for her husband, children, and, increasingly, all three living parents. As she watches younger coworkers move in and out of positions in her company every several years, María still feels anxiety about job uncertainty, despite her long tenure with her employer, as she is concerned about her lack of technological skills. She expends a lot of energy worrying about whether she should seek out other job opportunities in a less expensive living community, but she wonders if seeking change wouldn't just create greater instability and uncertainty. Moving would force her to leave familiar friends, community, and service providers behind. Making such a decision is heavily influenced by health insurance repercussions because it is scary to think about maintaining health insurance until she and her husband reach Medicare eligibility at age sixty-five. From all surface appearances, María seems to be living the American Dream, having reached a solid upper-middle-class economic status with a good job, a home, and college-educated children. Yet she and her husband feel themselves being tugged at both ends and worry about long-term economic stability in retirement and the inevitable increases in their cost of healthcare as they age. María can see all the moving parts and has diligently done all the "right things" to achieve the American Dream success formula throughout her life but doesn't have the time or expertise to organize all the puzzle pieces of her situation.

Sam

Sam is a Millennial in his early years in the workplace. His education has allowed him to earn income in a gig economy job using his computer programming skills. He is still single. Frankly, Sam doesn't pay much attention to his health in any overt way, although he likes eating at quick food establishments that say they serve organic foods. He doesn't have a primary care physician; rather, he goes to urgent care if absolutely necessary. He listened to his parents and obtained health insurance through his state's insurance exchange, although he was only willing to pay for the bronze plan. He mostly sees the sickcare system as either rarely applying to his life or capable of exponential scientific breakthroughs that might make any future health conditions solvable. He spends many hours a day playing video games and has only recently begun to notice that he huffs and puffs a bit when he walks up two or more flights of stairs. He vaguely notices that he drinks two to three beers almost every night. While he makes an above-average income for his age, he has no real savings and a significant amount of student loan debt. He did recently spend money on a popular genetic test to learn more about his genome and why he can pee after eating asparagus with no unusual odor. He is confident in his ability to maintain employment because everybody seems to need computer programmers and the company he provides services to keeps communicating how important he and his colleagues are. Nonetheless, he keeps a posting out on a job site in case a better option comes along. Sam is graced with the innocence and vitality of youth and takes his health for granted.

Segmentation Is Inadequate: Personalization Is Required

Why have I painted these portraits? Let me assure you it was not to depress you but rather to inspire your thinking! You might even be thinking that the descriptions of Sara, Fred, María, and Sam are pretty incomplete and that there is so much more you would want to know about them. Herein lies a conundrum! I've already offered far more detail than the sickcare system players, and the current information systems that support them, are designed to handle. As a result, the current healthcare system would place each of these individuals into segments according to their incumbent business models. These segments, to be clear, are probably best viewed as necessary but insufficient.

Health insurance companies, with a lens on benefit plans, would segment Sarah as a high-needs Medicaid beneficiary, and her kids would likely be part of the Children's Health Insurance Program (CHIP). Fred would be labeled a "senior" Medicare beneficiary who is approaching frail and elderly status, and his wife might require a SNP, or special needs plan. María is an employer-based commercially insured beneficiary with a spouse and two dependent children and a vehicle they can use to entice her parents into their Medicare Advantage plan. Sam is viewed as an individual commercially insured beneficiary with no dependents. The entities that provide health insurance would be continuously analyzing the revenue opportunities and cost risks for each of these individuals (i.e., the underwriting risks) to understand how to best design benefits programs for them and similar types of people.

Hospitals, with a different lens focused on delivering healthcare services, would view Sarah as being a prospect for birth and delivery with poor reimbursement characteristics; Fred as a hip or knee replacement waiting to happen with a wife who will require significant neurological care; María as a person to ply with pre-diabetes education and programming that would encourage her to use clinical services for her Medicare-participating parents; and Sam as a prospect for their urgent care centers and a potential sports medicine patient.

Today's healthcare industry players have to create such segments, or they can't function as systems. We'll dive deeper into the impacts and practicality of these segments in chapter 3. But for now, let's just make the point that ideally our healthcare system would first increase its understanding and then never lose sight of the individual as a total person. Of course, we rarely live in an ideal world.

Before we further explore how to optimize health, let me drive home the importance of personalization versus segmentation. All you have to do is change just one variable about each of our four persons to see a profound impact. Give Sarah a dependable daily caregiver for her children; Fred, a caring daughter with some time availability who lives in the same city; María, a husband with a substance abuse problem; and Sam, a chronic illness that causes him significant physical pain. Can you see how these simple variations shift the entire equation? Think about such shifts in these four lives as you read the equation again:

$$H_v = \frac{\textit{Health Status (person or population)}}{\textit{Clinical Care} + \textit{Daily Living}}$$

Before we leave the setup topic of variables in daily living, it must be emphatically pointed out that the individual person (i.e., the healthcare consumer) carries the major responsibility for the actions they take in their daily lives. Therefore, we must face another simple reality. Systems that are intended to get people to alter behaviors or take actions in pursuit of a goal, such as improved health status, generally do not work if people don't get incented and rewarded. We'll discuss that more in chapters 2 through 4.

I hope it's becoming obvious how woefully inadequate the sickcare system is to meet the diverse needs of our four consumers in a holistic way. To be fair to our healthcare system, it wasn't designed to do so. Beyond illustrating a diversity of healthcare needs, health benefit types, financial statuses, and lifestyles, the programs and resources that each of these individuals might best utilize to attain health optimization are also different. The one thing common to all of them is that the tools and access to resources they could use to make themselves healthier are fragmented. Each of the four consumers would benefit from the availability of a systematic approach of matching health improvement resources that could influence their total well-being and lessen their dependency on the sickcare system now and into their futures.

While we are all unique individuals with high variability in the factors that impact our daily living, I think it's fair to say that we all would like to be as healthy as possible. We're probably also united in the realization that our ability to be healthy in turn allows us to do the things we love and spend time with the people we love. What we all deserve is a personalized system of resources adaptable to our individual health and lifestyle needs … a system that helps us achieve our optimal health and total well-being.

While we are all unique individuals with high variability in the factors that impact our daily living, I think it's fair to say that we all would like to be as healthy as possible.

CHAPTER 2

UNDERSTANDING HEALTH OPTIMIZATION

Remember the old childhood rhyme your mother or grandmother may have used: "An apple a day keeps the doctor away"? Well, while eating a balanced daily portion of whole fruits is important to good health, it turns out the far better advice might be "Don't smoke that cigarette" or "Don't eat only processed foods." How about this one? "Don't be born into poverty." It's hard to have total well-being if you can't afford quality food or don't have a safe and reliable way to get to your job. Put our lives on a balance scale and the real deciders of good health weigh far heavier on lifestyle choices and environment than on what can be accomplished by the sickcare system.

Consider the definition from the World Health Organization of social determinants of health: "The conditions in which people live, learn, work, and play." Now recall the figure that weighed so heavily in the last chapter: 70 percent of your health is determined by factors outside clinical care and also beyond the fortune, or misfortune, of your genetics. Let's explore that a bit more. Beyond clichés about apples or constant reminders about consuming fresh fruits and vegetables, there are numerous physical, mental, social, financial, and self-identity components that impact your total health status. So while achieving optimal health might include something like having access to relevant nutrition counseling, that would be only *one* of numerous contributing elements. It might also include sleep improvement resources or a smoking cessation program or, thinking more broadly, enough money to move to a safer neighborhood with better schools and cleaner air. Any one such alteration could help make you healthier, but none of us can be wholly defined by only one aspect of our daily lives. We must think across the spectrum of which health improvement resources, including both clinical *and* daily living resources, a person needs and can actually access.

Health Optimization Requires Two-Axis Personalization

Bear with me as I finish out the setup of the unifying equation that underlies this book and that will transform an industry. Let's pick up the equation from chapter 1.

$$H_v = \frac{\textit{Health Status (person or population)}}{\textit{Clinical Care + Daily Living}}$$

Looking at the denominator of the equation, there are two distinct drivers of health status—clinical care and daily living. As silly as it may sound at first, give some thought to the familiar words I quoted from the traditional wedding vow as an epigraph for part I: "in sickness *and* in health." The emphasis I've placed on the word "and" in the vow is intended to ensure that we don't forget about the pursuit of improving health. In part, it also reflects that there's a great deal of good in the current healthcare system. Sickcare, in short, is very good at helping sick people. Focusing on the word "and" from the wedding vow underscores an important fundamental of this book's approach. How can we take what is best in the sickcare system we've inherited *and* marry it, if you will pardon the pun, to a holistic vision of health?

My previous book, *The Healthcare Cure,* enumerates in detail how we have arrived at inheriting the healthcare system—and the sickcare system at its heart—we currently have in place in this country. We simply don't have the luxury of revising the past and starting from scratch to get to a better future! What we must do instead is examine what works best in our current system, including the extremely high quality of our clinical care infrastructure and the exceptional level of research and development that results in the achievement of breakthrough therapies, treatments, and medicines. Then we need to expend even greater energy on analyzing where the current system fails, focusing particularly on its frequent inability to integrate other daily living drivers of health status with the clinical drivers for you, me, and every other person.

Achieving health optimization requires empowering consumers to take action in partnership with their healthcare providers to support all aspects of their health status around and *between* clinical care episodes. At the center of such a partnership is a vision of the consumer as a whole person, not just someone a health professional sees when they are sick. Thinking about Sarah, Fred, María, and Sam, none of them can be their healthiest and happiest without daily living factors like the economics that help shape the environment they live in, the presence of support systems such as quality caregivers and helpful family members, and their lifestyle habits and choices relating to levels of physical activity, what they eat and drink, and the like.

Thinking about how to depict the integration of clinical care and daily living in a useful framework, I introduced a concept to the healthcare industry that I call two-axis personalization. If there is one thing I've learned in thirty-five years of business, it's that if you are going to have success at creating change, you need a simple picture that, as the saying goes, is worth a thousand words. The following picture of two-axis personalization depicts the clinical care dimension on the vertical y-axis and the daily living dimension on the horizontal x-axis:

The Future of Healthcare Is Two-Axis Personalizaton
Seamlessly Integrating Clinical Resources with Consumer Resources

First, let's start with the vertical y-axis. As previously stated, it is widely accepted that approximately 30 percent (or less) of what drives our health is the quality of clinical care we receive. The healthcare industry today already thinks beyond the current methods for clinical prevention, diagnoses, and treatment and is endeavoring to take the best of what is currently known and make it better through the application of what is often called *personalized medicine*. Some also call it precision medicine. Personalized medicine is just as it sounds—moving clinical science well beyond the typical biometrics and lab testing inputs used today to diagnose and treat. By applying rapidly advancing biological science combined with the ability to manipulate huge data sets, precise and personalized treatments for individuals can be discerned based on that person's genomic, microbiomic, metabolomic, proteomic, glucomic, and epigenomic properties. Developing an understanding of "omics" and how therapies can be made increasingly effective are generally the domain of clinical and biomedical experts. The knowledge from research is transmitted to physicians and other clinical professionals through conventional teaching and publications, and with increasing frequency through the application of artificial intelligence (AI) tools that essentially assist the clinician in determining how to best apply the available knowledge to the clinical care of their patient. There is little doubt that physical, biological, and chemical science will continue to advance and develop new compounds, biologics, targeted gene therapies, vaccines, and other wondrous breakthroughs to treat and prevent illness. But do not underestimate the complexity of how challenging it is and will continue to be—even with assistance from AI—for clinicians to apply rapidly advancing medical technologies and the personalization of our individual "omics" to drive the best clinical care. And more importantly in the context of this book, keep in mind that even if clinical care with precision medicine is "perfected" in its accuracy and distribution, it still drives less than 30 percent of the health status for individuals and populations. This realization is difficult to wrap our heads around as we think about the binary, live-or-die nature of frightening illnesses such as COVID-19, certain types of cancers, rapid degenerative diseases, strokes, heart attacks, and so on. Nonetheless, most people spend most of their time living as consumers, not patients. And helping the many achieve and sustain their highest health status is an objective that must coexist with our understandable fascination with curing disease.

This takes us to the horizontal or *x*-axis. Again, it is widely accepted and understood that our daily living activities and environment drive 70 percent (or more) of our health status. Our daily living doesn't typically change abruptly with a visit to a doctor. It is unlikely that there will be a pill or injection that allows us to live in a different location, transports us safely from one place to another, makes nutritious food appear on our doorstep, becomes a substitute for exercise, educates us, or gets us a better job. You get the picture. Daily living is, well, daily living. Most of this book is about how we can systematically understand and apply technology and resources to positively impact the components of daily living of individual consumers, but always with a profound amount of respect for the importance of clinical care. Before we move ahead, however, it is critical to address a term that has made its way into the vernacular of the healthcare industry, and that is the term "social determinants." Current and future literature, studies, and "experts" will keep refining the definition and subclassifications of social determinants of health (SDoH). That's okay, as there are good reasons to debate approaches to housing, education, environment, and other factors that nearly all would agree impact our health. We will explore SDoH in more detail in chapter 6, but I need to make an important systematic point as it relates to the equation we have been developing.

At the risk of scaring every algebra-hating reader away from this book, the point I want to make is that SDoH is a coefficient or a multiplier to the components of daily living. In other words, water supply and food supply are examples of variable components of daily living. If the water supply is poor, like what occurred in Flint, Michigan, then that is a low-value environmental multiplier on health. If the water supply is clean and mineralized, as we might idealistically imagine is the case in a picturesque high mountain village, then it is a high-value multiplier. If we look at the classic example of good availability of fresh fruits and vegetables in a local food supply versus so-called "food deserts" where such things are hard to come by, you can apply the same logic. Think of it this way—each variable component you are trying to understand about a person in daily living ranges from very poor to excellent in terms of its impact on health. We are not going to spend time in this book assigning values because the industry doesn't even have the categories and components organized yet. But it's important that you understand that the components of daily living as impacted by SDoH are not just "good" or "bad." For example, a person can eat no fresh vegetables, a few fresh vegetables, some fresh vegetables, lots of fresh vegetables, and so on. The same is true in frequency, length, and types of exercise, social relationships, and the like. The point is that daily living components are generally not all or nothing, the way in which SDoH impact daily living is variable, and at a moment's notice, SDoH can change.

With a basic description of the clinical y-axis and the daily living x-axis, allow me to further advance the equation that started so simply:

$$H_v = \frac{\textit{Health Status (person or population)}}{\textit{Clinical Care ("omics")} + \textit{Daily Living (SDoH)}}$$

What this equation now tells us is that the clinical care components are significantly impacted by "omics" and daily living components are significantly impacted by SDoH. Some might read this and say that this is oversimplified because, for example, economic social determinants or language barriers might prevent a person from accessing clinical care. While this is hard to argue with, you will see that this book acknowledges these challenges while explaining how the healthcare system we have in place allows for ways to address these concerns based on the equation above. And, by the way, it is my hope that others grab this equation, rip it apart, and improve it. First, however, people should give thought to the massive amount of data types that describe health status, clinical care, and daily living, and then think about how the biggest data sets in existence are "omics" and, increasingly, multivariate data sets that map the relationship between social determinants, daily living, and health. There is much work to be done to apply the healthcare value equation to over 330 million people in the United States and over 7.5 billion in the world, but based on my thirty-five years of experience, I believe it is a unifying equation for creating a practical systematic framework for transforming our healthcare system.

> I believe it is a unifying equation for creating a practical systematic framework for transforming our healthcare system.

Feeling overwhelmed? So are most people who work in the industry! Please know that this book will only lightly touch upon the clinical care component of the denominator that impacts 30 percent of our health status, as this is where most other efforts in our industry have focused and it is certainly not my area of highest expertise. But the essential "missing piece" in massively transforming healthcare to be higher value is what remains in that denominator—daily living as impacted by the social determinants of health. As we think about Sarah, Fred, María, and Sam in their daily lives, we will develop a method for understanding the ways we can change the system to make them healthier at a lower cost.

We Can't Alter Time: We Can Apply Health Optimization Longitudinally

When we think about daily living, it's natural to think about time. Over the course of my lifetime, the concepts that define time have certainly expanded. I'm no physicist, but at one end of the time spectrum we have become accustomed to expressing universal events and objects in terms of "lightyears" of distance, with apparent accuracy, and dating earthly things across a range of billions of years. This makes the length of our lifetimes or a year within our lifetimes seem relatively small. On the other end of the spectrum, we have developed technology that allows us to slice time into tiny fragments, such as computer chips that can process billions of instructions per second with the promise of quantum computing about to move that beyond trillions per second. The computational science that allows us to analyze large amounts of data and execute instructions in small amounts of time is already helpful to all of us and is progressing at a rate that nearly ensures that it can be applied to both improving our health status and prolonging the length of our lives. As it relates to time and our ability to optimize our health and total well-being, let's think longitudinally about a person's time between birth and death and how we can apply our two-axis systematic framework and unifying equation for healthcare value.

By now it is probably common sense to you that our system of reactive sickcare is very weak at promoting long-term health and reducing morbidity (e.g., illness). Again, it is there to fix what ails us, with some notable exceptions of vaccines and public health measures (e.g., water and sewer services) that are meant to reduce disease occurrence in the general population. It's also important to understand the lingo pertinent to when you or I interact with the clinical healthcare system. When you have an acute illness or injury and undergo a medical or dental visit or procedure, that is called an episode. Episodes can get a bit complicated, but it's not necessary to break down an episode for the purposes of this book. What you need to understand is that for most of us, our interactions with the clinical healthcare system are episodic, and again, if you ascribed 1 percent of your time in a year (or approximately ninety hours) to these, that would be more time than most people spend in a typical year—even if you tack on all the time spent in waiting rooms. Thus, most of our time is spent in between episodic interactions with clinical resources.

If we take a typical longitudinal view of people across their lifetime for an entire population and chart it on a graph, we'll see a morbidity curve that is largely similar among most of us. In showing this curve, I do not mean to be insensitive to the many things that can happen to people that unfortunately cut lives short. But from a systematic point of view, I believe we will be better able to tackle those sorts of things by driving better health at lower costs into the bulk of the population.

The chart below illustrates the typical morbidity curve as we move through life, and it is meant to be conceptual, not precisely mathematical:

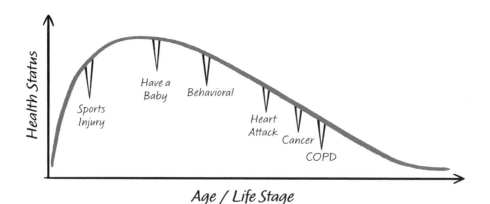

Hopefully the chart is easy to follow. We are born, and most people, for obvious biological reasons, attain their optimal physical health (i.e., their prime) from their late teens into their early twenties. Pick your favorite professional sport, look up the average age of participants, and you'll see a parallel. Most people hold relatively good health for a decade or so, and then as we age, our morbidity curve descends as we suffer episodic health events and the wear and tear of life and chronic illnesses accumulates. As we continue to move along in time and age, these physical health factors make us increasingly frail. The 2020 coronavirus pandemic, sadly, is an explicit example of how relatively poorly people over sixty years of age were able to withstand COVID-19 in contrast to those who were younger.

If we placed our representative consumers on the graph, Sam, our Millennial, although he has had infrequent interaction with the sickcare system and does little in the way of disease prevention or altering his sedentary lifestyle, is the closest to optimal health. Sam simply benefits from being young.

Fred, by contrast, is on the right side of the graph by virtue of his life stage and the increased likelihood of experiencing a significant acute health episode. But what could happen if we created a system that helped improve Fred's health status and lengthened and enriched his life and whose systematic principles also supported Sam's ability to sustain prolonged good health?

There are two ways to change the decline rate of the morbidity curve. Based on the equation, you have already guessed that you can affect health optimization through clinical resources *and* through daily living via resources that support health and total well-being. We will examine daily living resources further in chapters 6 and 11, as we dive deeper into a systematic framework for supporting optimal health. But for now it's important to understand that health optimization is not something the sickcare system can do alone. That system is very good at fixing us when we are sick or injured, mediocre at helping us prevent illness and injury, and downright poor at helping us address the life choices we can control that would make us healthier. Again, the time in between our clinical episodes of care is, well, most of the time. How can we use that time to flatten the decline in the morbidity curve or even, if you want to be ambitious, bend it upward and improve your health status at any age? To answer this question, you have to believe that you, as a person, can put the time you control to good use in an active and purposeful way as it relates to your health.

Health Optimization Is Quality Improvement for Humans

In every other industry I've encountered, quality occurs when processes are designed that are comprehensive regarding producing a good or service and ensure that errors or defects are eliminated as early in the set of processes as possible. There are a lot of factors that contribute to why the cost of your laptop computer or your television is going down even while its quality is going up, but among them are things like the supply chain management of the electronic components, elimination of unnecessary variation in the manufacturing process, testing prior to product release, and workforce training. The essential question is this: What if we shifted our attention from only taking care of people once

> *What if we shifted our attention from only taking care of people once they are sick to creating processes that help people take actions that elevate their health across the whole of their lives?*

40

they are sick to creating processes that help people take actions that elevate their health across the whole of their lives? My primary professional goal is to help create such systems, ones that can have a direct impact on the quality of people's health and as a natural offshoot of doing so positively impact their overall quality of life.

The details of what makes up a life can be quite different for each of us, but we can all take steps toward health optimization. In the chart below, let's assume that Sam and Fred have similar genetic traits and plot them at different times on the same morbidity curve. Let's assume that María began life with a bit more fortuitous set of environmental and genetic traits, and let's assume that Sarah grew up with a set of circumstances that deprived her of early-life nutrition and imposed other negative environmental factors, so that her peak health did not quite hit its full potential. The point is this: While we all have different morbidity curves, nonetheless we each have our own morbidity curve—from birth to death. That means that no matter what your curve, or where you are on that curve, you have an opportunity to improve your health status and/or delay its decline in all but the most unfortunate circumstances.

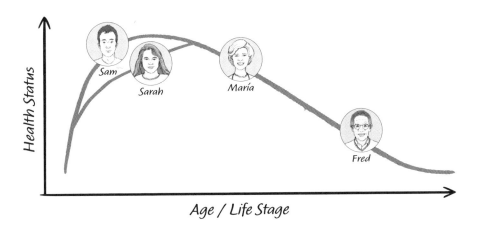

Because of the very nature of the healthcare industry, value isn't only a matter of economic cost, but it is also a measure of cost for quality—certainly of the quality of an individual's health. Just like in manufacturing, where quality processes produce a better "product" at a lower cost, in this case the product is human beings who are living at their highest possible health and well-being status at a lower cost.

The unifying healthcare value equation we have discussed allows us to systematically operationalize quality in both clinical care and daily living. For example, preventive clinical measures like vaccinations and health literacy programming in nutrition and fitness as early as possible in the sequence of a person's life are relatively low-cost health improvement resource inputs to health with high value. In general, the costs to provide health improvement resources for daily living are much lower than clinical care health improvement resources. For example, while there is currently a fascination with telemedicine as an input to the clinical care component of the denominator—and telemedicine is a positive and convenient step for consumers to be sure—it is only slightly lower cost than traditional visits, and the actual value-producing interaction still requires roughly the same human face-to-face time. By contrast, many of the types of resources that can positively impact daily living are available in the form of software and data-driven programs that can be available and relevant 24-7 and in which each interaction can cost a fraction of a penny. What's so powerful about this is that just like the cost of computing power and storage have declined as technology advances, in healthcare the total costs can go down even while the frequency of touches to a person increases as we apply the power of information technology. Some types of resources may not be totally digital and still require humans on the other end, but by notifying consumers about the resources, matching consumers to the correct resources, assisting with enrollment and scheduling of those resources, and making it easy to complete actions within and across a range of resources, far greater efficiency can be realized than that of today's hit-or-miss, fragmented reality. This systematically produces the added benefit of freeing up clinicians to spend more time with those who have greater medical needs, not to mention more time to personalize our own care when we do utilize their services.

We will discuss more how to accomplish quality through health optimization throughout this book, but I hope it is clear that by lining up a personalized array of resources that support and reward the actions we take, tailored to the whole of a person's needs and taking their SDoH into consideration, we can minimize the need for sickcare and drive higher quality and value. The result of consumers taking actions to improve their health between episodes can change the morbidity curve, as in the illustration below, saving cost and improving health.

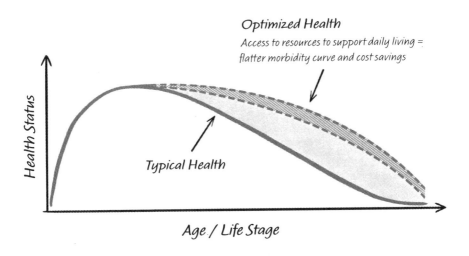

Now, you may be saying, "I get how we can help younger and middle-aged people, but I'm not too excited about the right end of the diagram!" Well, I have good news for you. Let's return to Fred to help illustrate how health optimization can be applied at any time. What are Fred's needs? We know that he is the caregiver for his wife. But what are other needs he has that, if addressed, could create a higher quality of life and translate to better overall health? He certainly has nutritional needs that if addressed will help maintain his biological health and, in his case, reduce the hemoglobin A1C levels that currently make him a borderline diabetic. He will benefit from exercise programs that focus on things like maintaining balance to reduce falls. That exercise, combined with clinical care from his physician, can actually reverse his level of cardiovascular disease. Accordingly, he can reduce the chance of stroke. He would benefit from financial counseling that lowers his stress. Through online connection to a support group of others who take care of spouses with dementia, he could build resiliency and lower his chance of becoming depressed. He could have an app on his phone that helps him track and administer his and his wife's prescriptions or schedule medical appointments. If Fred has ready access to such resources, do you honestly doubt that he will realize an improvement in the quality of his mental and physical health? Even at his advanced age, is it not likely that such improvements might delay or mitigate some of his future dependency on the costly resources the sickcare system might provide? The next picture illustrates how Fred's morbidity curve can be bent upward.

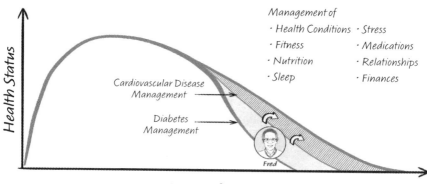

I almost hope at this point you are saying, "Duh ... this is obvious; let's do it!" If so, I hope you are asking yourself why such obviousness is not put into place for all of our senior citizens. The answer to that question will reveal itself as we move through this book, but suffice it to say that the platform that would allow Fred to easily navigate both sickcare and daily living resources does not widely exist, yet.

At this point, please forgive me for not stepping through examples for Sarah, María, and Sam as I just did for Fred. We need to move on to understanding how we can accomplish two-axis personalization and flatten and/or improve people's morbidity curves. But I have included similar discussions for the other three individuals in the conclusion.

We Can All Become the Healthiest (i.e., "Optimized") Versions of Ourselves

I am confident we can help individuals like Fred discover improved physical, mental, and social health within his financial constraints. And without going into great detail now, I hope it's clear that for Sam, Sarah, and María, health optimization can become truly transformative. For just like with all forms of quality improvement processes, the closer to the source you can implement it—in Sam's case, at the youngest age possible—the higher the results that can be produced at a lower cost. When we can systematically understand the holistic realities of these four lives, we can begin to realize that there is an enormous opportunity to both improve the effectiveness of sickcare episodes and better manage in-between episodes while improving overall health, happiness, and quality of life.

This is where we come back to that *and* I talked about early in this chapter. Rather than remove the best of what the sickcare system can offer, health optimization envisions an approach that takes the 30 percent of our health status best treated by the sickcare system and links it to the 70 percent of our health status that is determined by lifestyle and environment.

Optimization is not the same thing as perfection. We will never realize perfection in healthcare.

Optimization is not the same thing as perfection. We will never realize perfection in healthcare. In fact, the very nature of biology suggests perfection is impossible— but we *can* make everyone their healthiest. To do so means we must first be honest with ourselves about the emphasis we currently place on a system focused almost entirely on sick people and how we pay for it.

Part II: For Richer, for Poorer

Enriching Consumer Resources across Health Benefits

CHAPTER 3

IF YOU DON'T START WITH BENEFITS DESIGN, YOU CAN'T FIX THE SICKCARE SYSTEM

There's a famous anecdote from Bill Clinton's 1992 presidential election campaign in which his campaign manager, James Carville, hung a sign in their headquarters that read, "It's the economy, stupid!" The sign was a visible and constant reminder of the path required for an election win. The phrase "It's the economy, stupid" has been part of the common vernacular ever since, and the word "economy" regularly gets replaced by some other central concept. In similar fashion we can't talk about shifting the focus from sickcare to health optimization without understanding the consumer face of healthcare economics—specifically, that our access to services and providers is primarily determined by the benefits segment of which we are a part. In the world of healthcare, "It's the benefits, stupid!"

Ironically, that handwritten campaign sign from nearly thirty years ago wasn't only about the economy; it had two other lines long forgotten by most—the second highlighting the need for change and the third stating, "Don't forget healthcare." This is a good reminder that we have been trying to find a fix for what ails our healthcare system for a good long while. The consumer-facing core of the sickcare system operates on an unusual economic model. How we pay for our healthcare is determined by the benefit system of which we are a part. Benefit systems are complex bundles of rules and resources. And benefits systems bear little similarity to how we typically exchange goods and services when we shop online or make purchases at our local big-box store. In those venues we can compare models, shop prices, and read reviews before making a simple, direct transaction at a visible price. In the sickcare system, it might be nearly impossible to know the actual price of the service, procedure, or pill, and your options to shop the competition will be limited. In paying for the service, you'll embark on a bureaucratic expedition of navigating the rules and procedures of your health benefits system. In sickcare it's not so much "How much do I owe?" as it is "Who and how much do I pay once I learn how much is covered by my insurance?" It's a rare transaction when you walk up to a cash register and pay a full, posted price directly to the provider. Imagine trying to buy groceries and learning that the price you pay for a loaf of bread is different from what someone else pays at the same store, in the same line, and then imagine that if you file all the proper paperwork, some other entity will be picking up a portion of the price— with all this transpiring at a later date.

It's the centrality of benefit plans that we must comprehend if we are going to move toward a system that optimizes health and engages ordinary consumers.

Benefits programs are simply a mysterious world for most of us. Yet it's the centrality of benefit plans that we must comprehend if we are going to move toward a system that optimizes health and engages ordinary consumers. If we fail to understand the benefits segments that govern what services you can access and what portion of those services you ultimately pay for out-of-pocket, we cannot talk about change to the system. Without such an anchoring, we don't really even have a starting point from which we can begin to add an ecosystem of daily living resources that improve health.

Health Benefits Basics

The segmented constructs of benefits in the United States are based on economics, job status, and age. The basic premise of health insurance in the United States is a system of benefits that define the rules by which a person can access doctors, hospitals, pharmaceuticals, and medical supplies. It also determines what portion of payment for those services and goods will be the responsibility of the consumer and what portion will be the responsibility of the insurance provider.

Now, if we leave healthcare out of the equation and consider other forms of insurance—think of all the other stuff that can maim us, kill us, or destroy our property, like fires and floods—we begin to think of insurance as something that protects us from catastrophic loss. It's what you turn to when your house burns down or your teenager wrecks your car. In those instances we file a claim and are issued a check that we can then use to find a contractor or body shop we want to do the repair work.

By contrast, health insurance has come to mean the way we pay for healthcare goods and services. Your health insurance doesn't feel like coverage for loss—even to cover that catastrophic injury, such as when your ACL unexpectedly proved weaker than the rest of your body—rather, health insurance feels like the means by which you pay for your doctors, prescriptions, lab and imaging tests, and usage of the emergency room or hospital. Or, put into daily living terms related to financial health, conscious thinking about health insurance most often comes into people's minds upon the first instance of paying for those medical services. Some interactions are more retail oriented, like going to the pharmacy counter. But for doctors, diagnostics, and hospitals, you later get a hefty bill stating, "You owe your provider $X,XXX. XX; your insurance has already paid its portion." This amount you owe is called the "out-of-pocket" cost and also can be referred to as first-dollar payment. Because of a lack of understanding about health benefits, many people generally think if they have health insurance that somebody or something else is going to pay for *all* their access to care. Because of the complexities of benefit system payments, one common industry term used today is "surprise billing," which is generally used to describe that a person did not know or understand that healthcare would actually cost them out-of-pocket. Even for those who fully comprehend that they will owe "something," discerning how much is further complicated because health insurers operate under negotiated rates and don't typically pay the full amount requested by the provider for a visit, procedure, or prescription.

There once was an era in the United States when people with health insurance policies had relatively small deductibles and received payment to reimburse them when they went to the doctor, required a hospital stay, or garnered prescriptions. It didn't take an economist to realize that small deductibles couldn't carry the burden of the total health spend and that most consumers couldn't handle the responsibility of paying their medical providers in timely and accurate ways. In the early 1980s, we began to mature the concept of what is known as managed care, which essentially means that the person with the benefits coverage has a level of responsibility to follow certain rules and guidelines in order to access care and that they are getting help from another entity, usually a health plan, to determine where and how to best receive that care. The entity offering the health benefits plan negotiates the amount that the provider is going to be reimbursed for the delivery of goods and services. In return for volume and assurance of payment, the providers of healthcare services and goods negotiate discounts. And this principle is true whether the health insurance payer is for profit, like United Health Group; not for profit, like many local Blue Cross and Blue Shield plans; federal and state government programs like Medicare and Medicaid; or even self-funded employers who take on the payment risk for their employee populations. It makes sound business sense, but it also means that the concept of transparent pricing is nonsense. In other words, unless every doctor, dentist, pharmacy, lab, imaging center, and the like offers the exact same price to every health insurance payer, then the amount that your services and goods will cost is not something that can be published and have any meaning. Your price is determined by your benefit plan!

Of course, the reality of how this occurs is far more complex than it sounds here in principle. The purpose of this book is not to sort out those complexities. However, I need to lay a basic foundation for the anchoring points of today's benefits system. Only then can we have a common understanding as I talk about the way forward to making sure everyone has opportunities to realize better health. Political campaigns understand a key principle that seems to evade healthcare industry leaders: If we think we can make change happen without paying attention to people's wallets, we're fooling ourselves.

Benefits Building Blocks and Segments

Central to what we must understand are basic principles of how health benefits work and the common language we use to discuss them. Our current healthcare system is siloed to the extreme. The gulf between providers and benefit plan administrators, patients, hospital finance departments, and a dozen other codependent relationships is vast. Experts in one part of the system often know little about another part of the system, so having at least a common language regarding the essentials of the benefits system is vital. An entity or a person may well be an expert in one part of the broader industry and limited in its knowledge of another part. Think of the benefits manager at a commercial insurance company and the expertise they possess versus the expertise of a surgeon. Both may be superstars in their fields, and they may both work within the larger realm of "healthcare," but their expertise does not translate from one to the other. Bear with me as I offer a quick, generalized primer on the segments that make up the health benefits system and some of the terminology it uses.

Let's start with what might seem obvious, how the individual consumer gains access to the system: premiums. A *premium* is the amount paid on behalf of the person per month to provide the benefits coverage. Sometimes an individual pays all their own premium, sometimes an employer pays most or all of the premium, and sometimes the government pays most or all of the premium. One important note is that when the government pays providers directly for Medicare and Medicaid services, versus operating though a private health insurer, there is no actual premium—in other words, there is no accountable amount of revenue per person per month, which makes it very difficult to budget and manage. Having revenue to assign cost against is why there is good bipartisan support for both managed Medicare and managed Medicaid.

When accessing care, the consumer must often pay a *deductible*, the amount that has to be paid out-of-pocket before the insurance benefits kick in to pay the balance. This is more parallel to our expectations from other insurance, like that pertaining to the fender bender your teenager had, which cost you a deductible before the policy picked up the rest.

Depending on the specific requirements of the plan, individuals are also likely required to make a copayment at the time of service. *Copayments* are generally nominal payments or percentage payments (called *coinsurance*) that a consumer has to make to receive medical services or get a prescription. The purpose of a copayment is to remind you that the health goods and services you access actually cost real money. Having your employer withhold your contribution to your benefits plan from your paycheck can seem to camouflage the financial exchange going on behind the scenes, so copayments are a kind of reminder that you're paying for something. They're also in place to discourage you from overusing resources and, of course, to burden you and your family with some portion of the economic responsibility. At twenty-five or fifty dollars a transaction or at 30 percent of the cost, you might think twice about visiting your doctor for what you believe are probably seasonal allergies.

Most of us gain access to the care we need through a provider network. The *provider network* is a curated list of doctors, hospitals, pharmacies, labs, or medical suppliers within an approved network in the healthcare supply chain. The network has already negotiated pricing with the health insurance payer on behalf of its provider members. The purpose of such networks, from a benefits design point of view, is to encourage people to stay within that designated network in order to control costs and maintain quality of care.

The typical health benefits plan will feature a *maximum out-of-pocket* amount, which is exactly what the term implies: the total highest amount per individual or per family that you would have to pay in a given year. The maximum out-of-pocket cap is the one feature of health benefits that echoes how we think of other insurance—putting a limitation on your total risk. And somewhat in parallel to the protection you get from the maximum out-of-pocket amount, your insurer is protected by the *maximum benefit* assigned to your policy. This is the highest amount that the insurance company would be responsible for paying. If your maximum out-of-pocket cost might keep you from going bankrupt after a catastrophic health episode, the maximum benefit is there to make sure the insurance company doesn't go out of business.

Now, needless to say, there is a great deal of nuance within the applications of all these terms. But they all apply to the various segments into which people are divided in the health benefits system, even if the particulars of those plans are different. Let's talk about those segments, at least in the most basic terms of what they are and whom they serve. We have to understand them if we are to see a path forward beyond the current limitations of the sickcare system because, again, for all insured individuals, the economics that drive the behaviors of the healthcare system start here.

Commercial Group Health Insurance

This is when an employer offers subsidized health insurance to an employee and their dependents as part of a total compensation package. In general, commercial insurance is made available to full-time employees, and the company pays a significant portion of the insurance premium, in essence sharing the cost of access to the healthcare system with the employee. Commercial policies are sold by both for-profit and not-for-profit health insurance companies. Sometimes the health insurance company takes on the risk for the cost of healthcare for their employees and dependents. Sometimes the employer takes on that risk in what is referred to as self-funded commercial insurance, where the insurance company provides the network of providers and administrative services only (ASO). The difference between a fully insured or self-funded plan is usually invisible to the employee, as they just know that they have a health insurance benefit and aren't concerned about the financing mechanism in the background. Most commercial health insurance benefit plans are structured as either a preferred provider organization (PPO) or health maintenance organization (HMO). The main difference is that an HMO requires patients to choose a primary care physician, who serves as the central provider and coordinates the care provided by specialists or other healthcare practitioners, creating the system many find annoying in which we await an appointment with an overbooked primary physician simply because we need a referral to a dermatologist, podiatrist, or urologist. PPOs, in contrast, often allow self-referral, so long as the specialist is within the approved provider network.

The employee-paid portion of the premium, along with out-of-pocket costs, represents one of the largest expenses undertaken by most median income families, often only exceeded by housing costs.

In 2018, 49 percent of Americans were covered by an employer-based commercial health plan.[3] Within such plans employers paid, on average, 82 percent of the benefit cost for single coverage (the employee) and 71 percent for family coverage.[4] Because the average cost of commercial insurance premiums for a family is somewhere in the neighborhood of $20,000, the employee-paid portion of the premium, along with out-of-pocket costs, represents one of the largest expenses undertaken by most median income families, often only exceeded by housing costs. Needless to say, employee insurance is also one of the large financial expenses an employer incurs and one reason some employers keep their number of employees who are eligible for health insurance closely in check. Because health benefits can be so expensive, many in the US workforce remain in lower-paying jobs precisely so that they can obtain health insurance benefits through their employer.

Working for a company that provides employee health insurance often has other benefits as well. Commercial insurance plans in larger employers tend to offer resources that can help you manage chronic diseases, cope with life challenges and stresses, and guide you toward useful, fairly priced resources; think of María having access to a family financial planning class or Sam having a discounted fitness program membership. This is a relatively new phenomenon, both suggesting incremental change among how employers see value in benefits and reflecting a need for greater competitive advantage for hiring and retaining employees. What might such resources look like? Well, among those who applied for consideration to the National Business Group on Health's annual "Best Employer" awards in 2018, 70 percent had smoke-free campuses, 72 percent offered time off to promote well-being activities, and 81 percent collected health metrics for their employees.[5] Such additional benefits are extremely attractive to many employees and can significantly improve total health if put to use. From the company perspective, your employer has an interest not only in you getting well when you're sick, but in keeping you healthy and productive. If you're working and producing, they may gain sufficient value to pay their part in keeping you that way.

Because conventional employer-provided commercial plans allow the employee to include his or her family, about half of America's children aged zero to eighteen are covered by commercial benefit plans. In 2018, 49 percent of children in the United States were covered under an employer-provided plan, with an additional 5 percent covered under privately purchased commercial plans.[6] Current regulations allow for dependents to be part of such plans until age twenty-six, essentially redefining the definition of "children."

Commercial Health Insurance
for Individuals and the Self-Employed

At present, with a continuing rise in the price of healthcare and a political interest, if a fractured one, in healthcare reform, many consumers now pay privately for benefit plans that bear much similarity to employer-provided packages. The Affordable Care Act (ACA) aimed to create the means for those who own small businesses or who work independently to access care through individual or small group insurance. The objective is to create larger insurance pools among those who are not employed by corporations or sizable companies. These plans are similar in design to commercial insurance plans purchased by large employers but are relatively very costly to those paying the premiums for two key reasons. First, there is no employer helping to pay part of the bill (although the government can step into that role and provide graduated subsidies based on income where some or all of the premium can be offset). Second, the risk pool for individuals and small businesses is more difficult to underwrite. If enough young people like Sam don't sign up to offset older, sicker people, it's a problem. Despite all of the frequently shared opinions about the merits or shortcomings of the ACA, for our purposes, we can cluster such individual and small group plans under the broader segment of commercial health insurance.

Medicaid

If you're not fortunate enough to hold a job or to work for an employer that offers health insurance, then in the United States you're eligible for Medicaid, so long as your income does not exceed an established threshold. Currently, that threshold is four times the poverty rate for an individual or for a family.[7] Medicaid programs are administered at the state level, although states apply to the federal government for support.

People who fall into this lower income segment often face SDoH issues beyond unemployment or underemployment that significantly impact their daily lives. Sarah is an example of someone who suffers the daily difficulties that plague many living at or near the poverty level, including environments that can threaten their safety, reduce their access to a quality food supply, make transportation difficult, place strains on their local schools, and limit opportunities for adult education that might move them ahead. People like Sarah can become trapped in vicious cycles. If Sarah can't afford a car and must rely on spotty public transportation, finding better-paying opportunities beyond walking or biking distance is problematic, particularly if what is available is shift work that requires a commute at hours that public transportation doesn't run or that further complicate the already difficult task of finding affordable, dependable childcare. With gentrification in and near city centers, which tends to push the impoverished to housing at greater distances from employers and governmental support services, such problems are only exacerbated. If Sarah lives in a food desert (defined by the US Department of Agriculture as neighborhoods that don't have access to a supermarket within a mile in urban areas or within twenty miles in rural areas[8]), her resulting dependence on cheap food or fast food expands her likelihood of acquiring chronic diseases like diabetes, increases her stress, lessens her energy, and compounds other existing health issues. For Medicaid recipients like Sarah, the likelihood of living in food deserts, particularly if they do not own a car, are high, a reality the US Department of Agriculture says impacts more than 4 percent of Americans.[9]

I haven't saddled Sarah or her children with mental illness or substance abuse in our illustration, yet the reality is, based on data representing others in this benefit cohort, I easily could have done so. Someone living in Sarah's neighborhood would be accustomed to regularly encountering those who suffer such conditions, as they are disproportionately present in impoverished urban environments. A brief issued by the Kaiser Foundation reported that Medicaid covered 21 percent of adults with mental illness, 26 percent of adults diagnosed as having a serious mental illness, and 17 percent of adults with a substance use disorder. To put this in perspective, Medicaid covered 14 percent of the general adult population.[10]

While such numbers of Medicaid recipients can be overwhelming, as can other statistical trends demonstrating high usage of the sickcare system's resources, one of the problems with a program like Medicaid is our tendency to paint the people making up this benefit segment with a broad brush. To do so isn't just unfair; it's dangerous. While someone like Sarah is useful to look at because she is representative of a lot of generalities applicable to others living in similar impoverished environments, to fail to see her as an individual with unique needs is to fail her. We've built a segmented system that reduces her access to healthcare as it is, but when we make stereotyped assumptions about her or don't recognize the systemic health and economic complications of living in what most of us would view as substandard conditions, we cannot address the needs that might offer her a better life. As distinct as her life and her needs are, Sarah represents the 21 percent of Americans who are dependent on Medicaid for access to health services.[11]

While states can administer Medicaid plans by themselves, the general trend is toward what is called managed Medicaid. Managed

Medicaid is when the same types of insurance companies that offer commercial insurance apply their expertise and bring principles of managed care to Medicaid. This is done in an attempt to ensure appropriate networks and resources are put in place in appropriate geographies to make it easier for high-needs individuals to gain access to services. If commercial health plans emphasize ways to keep employees happy and productive, Medicaid plans create resources to keep beneficiaries safe and functioning. It's nearly a bureaucratic application of Maslow's hierarchy of needs in action, covering the essential safety needs of lower-income populations but never developing the opportunities for self-actualization afforded those with greater financial freedom. As a result, the differences between the plans reflect the distinct perspectives their recipients often hold toward the access those plans grant. When an acute health episode hits, whether you are commercially insured or a Medicaid recipient, you hope that your plan provides you access to the experts who can make you better. But for all the remainder of your time, if you have access to care under an employer-provided commercial plan, you probably don't give its details much thought, allowing you to think about vacations and other lifestyle amenities that bring you happiness. If you rely on Medicaid for your access to care, your distractions when healthy are quite different, for much of your energy is directed to thinking about the basics of food and shelter and financial survival. While chronic conditions aren't treated tremendously differently from acute episodes in commercial and managed Medicaid plans, standard Medicaid recipients often face difficult barriers to accessing maintenance drugs, medical services, and behavioral health services.

Medicare

If you are fortunate enough to reach age sixty-five, or if you are younger but have some type of permanent illness that rises to a defined level of disability, then you're eligible for Medicare. The 1964 Medicare Act was, with the exception of the Social Security Act, the largest and easily the most significant social welfare legislation ever introduced in the United States. Its original intent was to make sure that elderly individuals, even if they were of limited economic means, would not go bankrupt paying for basic healthcare. In truth, however, most people think once we reach age sixty-five, the government is going to pay for our healthcare. And although we will face nominal fees, in our retirement years we are largely free from the worry of the cost burden of health insurance. As people live longer, the same comfort does not apply to how people might pay for assisted living and few people do financial planning with the understanding that there are limits to what Medicare can and will pay.

Just like Medicaid, Medicare comes in two flavors. Individual Medicare allows any individual who is eligible to be attended to by any doctor, hospital, or pharmacy that is Medicare approved. The other flavor is managed Medicare, where, once again, coherent networks of care and managed care processes are put in place to help support and guide the Medicare beneficiary into getting the right help at the right place at the right price.

Because of some of the core goals behind Medicare benefits, this segment dovetails quite nicely into a health optimization approach, as it can slow the rate of health decline and reverse illness or diseases where possible. And as we've already discussed, reversing disease with the proper individualized care *is* possible even for those in retirement. With affordable access to clinical care and daily living resources, we know that heart disease can be reversed, hemoglobin blood sugar levels can be brought under control, and loneliness can be addressed, just to name three common needs among the Medicare population.

While of minimal expense to its beneficiaries, Medicare is quite expensive to its administrator—the federal government. There's a bit of a Catch-22 here, for as we make people healthier for longer, they live longer, which means they use the benefits of Medicare longer. These expenses are accelerated because tremendous costs usually occur as people become frail, elderly, and near the end of life. It's become relatively rarer, with a noticeable change over the course of my lifetime, that people drop dead instantly of a massive coronary. Rather, the quality of sickcare we receive for the 30 percent of our total health driven by clinical care has become so good that people can survive illnesses and conditions and deterioration for years and even decades, something that was not possible fifty or a hundred years ago. It turns out, staying alive when you are old costs a lot of money. And it costs more money every year. In 2018 Medicare spending accounted for 15 percent of total federal spending, rising to $731 billion in benefit payments. Projections from the Congressional Budget Office and calculations from the Board of Medicare Trustees within the Centers for Medicare & Medicaid Services Office of the Actuary from 2019 forecast Medicare benefit payments will reach 18 percent of total federal spending by 2029.[12]

There's a third financial pressure on the Medicare system—an overall aging population. The US Census Bureau estimates that by 2050 the number of people who are sixty-five and older will be higher than those who are younger than eighteen.[13] Many have focused on America's aging because of the pressures it places on Social Security, a system established in an era when we couldn't expect a larger generation to live far longer than those that came before them. Of course, Medicare suffers the same burdens. Over the last three years, on average

Medicare provided health coverage to more than forty-nine million Americans or about 15 percent of the nation's population. Medicare enrollment is expected to reach sixty-four million in 2020 and eighty million in 2030.[14] It's not difficult math to see that fewer people paying into funding Medicare and more people accessing its benefits create a sustainability concern.

If Fred can continue to afford to keep a roof over his head, he has reasonably affordable access to the healthcare he and his wife need, at least to care for their chronic conditions and for when future catastrophic episodes occur. Will the Medicare benefits that provide Fred access to care continue to exist when María reaches Fred's age? How can any healthcare benefits system address the growing reality that financial hardship forces more and more elderly individuals to work, often at poor-paying hourly jobs, well beyond conventional retirement age? Those are questions for another book. The question for this book is: Does the current healthcare system treat Fred and María with the same processes, or can it more holistically recognize that they access care through quite different benefit experiences and need enriched benefits that are personalized to them as individuals?

VA and TRICARE

The two benefits programs for retired military, the Veteran's Administration (VA) and, for active military members, TRICARE, represent other government-organized benefit and delivery systems. Both benefits programs are funded through taxation rather than through premiums. Such a funding arrangement disconnects its benefits recipients from the real cost of care, which in turn can provide them little incentive to make decisions to control their use of care. The same can often be said of the providers and services to which they have access. If you were given a credit card and told you were not responsible for paying its balance, would you spend time reviewing what you charged? Because these benefits programs are paid for through taxation, one sticking point is that the appropriations of tax dollars have to keep up with the cost of healthcare inflation in order to maintain quality of service. Add to that the reality that many of our veterans have suffered significant physical injuries and been through levels of mental trauma that are, simply put, worse than what most people experience. That means the responsibility burden on our nation to take care of these people who made sacrifices for our country is high and that the clinical and other resource needs are relatively higher than the average, resulting in a high-cost population.

As of March 2019, there were 9.17 million veterans enrolled in the Veteran Affairs Healthcare System.[15] TRICARE serves about 9.4 million beneficiaries.[16] As we've seen in our headlines with regularity, VA and TRICARE have their own unique challenges and strengths. Yet both benefit from having their beneficiaries be part of integrated delivery systems that provide care in more localized environments, with patient populations of sufficient scale to justify the tremendous amount of infrastructure required to provide quality care and without facing competition from other providers. This last factor is something quite unique to these health systems tied to military service.

Segmentation Meets Personalization

Unless you are completely uninsured, you are a beneficiary in one of the segments I have just described. And while a health optimization approach can also be applied to the uninsured population with likely tremendous benefits to ease the burden for those individuals and for unreimbursed emergency rooms, that discussion is beyond the scope of this book because, in short, there is no benefit plan to serve as the anchoring point for those individuals.

If we're going to speak seriously about moving systematically beyond sickcare, we have to understand these segmented benefit plans, and we have to respect the traditions from which they have evolved.

Segment is the applicable word here, for each is a segment of the larger healthcare system. And just as every system is made up of components, it also faces constraints. The benefit plan type and design to which people are attached is the primary constraint in the model for achieving health optimization.

> The benefit plan type and design to which people are attached is the primary constraint in the model for achieving health optimization.

Realizing this is not only important in economic terms of what we are eligible to access, but it's also a good starting point for discussing the role of social determinants of health. While I have already warned of the risk of casting generalizations about the individuals who comprise any of the benefits segments, there are patterns within segment populations that are important to the solutions proposed by this book. Understanding that Sarah, because of her economic position and location, is less likely to have a higher education, more likely to have limitations on her access to healthy food, less likely to have reliable childcare, more likely to be dependent on public transportation—you get the picture of these matter-of-fact social determinants that are present in low-income environments—you at least have some basis for discussing the constraints common to the Medicaid segment. In turn, recognizing this reality about the relationship between economics and benefit segments can allow us a starting point to then engage Sarah, Sam, María, and Fred to find out more about their personalized needs and resource availability.

No matter what benefit plan we are discussing, the promise of health optimization says that there is a more intelligent way to curate a set of health improvement resources that are personalized and localized to the beneficiary and that are within the realistic constraints of the benefits segment. In short, we'd ask María and Sarah questions about the types of parenting resources they need in very different manners. This does not reflect assumptions about either of their parenting abilities but rather the financial SDoH realities that suggest Sarah may need to research how to enroll her daughter in a free or reduced-price school meal program, while María may be looking to apply for a student loan interest reduction. We need to use a different language, a different way of forming a question because their immediate needs are distinct. Most of the healthcare industry has tried to segment people as doctors would: by their health status—well, at risk, chronically ill. If we switch segmentation to the benefit type (which is always how we discuss the economic side of the industry regarding individuals) rather than the clinical designation, we're already way ahead in our knowledge of that person and what's accessible to them when it comes to improving their health. This certainly is not the way most doctors are trained. If we take a closer look at the denominator of the unifying equation here, we see that you need to include both clinical care and daily living in the definition of a benefit plan. In other words,

$$\frac{\text{Clinical Care}}{\text{Resources}} + \frac{\text{Daily Living}}{\text{Resources}} = \text{"The Benefit Plan"}$$

So if we look again at the unifying equation, unless we tailor both clinical care and daily living resources in a personalized manner in the context of benefit plans, we will not move the needle on achieving higher health status at a lower cost.

$$H_v = \frac{\text{Health Status } (\text{person or population})}{\text{Clinical Care } (\text{"omics"}) + \text{Daily Living } (\text{SDoH})}$$

Bear with me for an analogy. If you were at a car rental counter in the early 2000s and were presented with a Kia, you'd probably either start looking for an upgrade or for the hidden camera belonging to the television show that was pranking you. For years Kia languished at the bottom of the annual J. D. Power Initial Quality Study (IQS) results. Comedian Paul Varghese used to do a whole slew of Kia jokes, like this one: "The guy at the rental counter said, 'Sir, we upgraded you … to a Kia.'" The punchline: "You upgraded me from what, shoes?" Yet in 2016 and 2017 Kia ascended

Unless we tailor both clinical care and daily living resources in a personalized manner in the context of benefit plans, we will not move the needle on achieving higher health status at a lower cost.

all the way to a number one ranking on the IQS survey.[17] Kia cars are now known as safe and reliable, and for that matter increasingly are seen as sporty and well appointed. Now, no one is going to mistake a Kia Rio for any high-end model manufactured by Mercedes-Benz, BMW, or Lexus. Nor is your Rio going to sport all their luxury features. So okay, the Kia dealership probably isn't even on the same street as those luxury car companies, but then that's kind of the point. Just because you're paying a fraction of the cost someone with more means is paying doesn't mean you can't have a dependable, safe car that not only gets you from point A to point B but also may just be a pleasure to drive. A lot of the health resources Sarah needs are entirely different from what Sam needs (or wants), but rather than reduce the quality of Sarah's care, why not personalize it to something that provides her the greatest benefit? This kind of personalization based on her situation can quite literally improve her health. And doesn't Sarah deserve quality in the resources available to her every bit as much as Sam does? Like the Kia example, we can achieve quality without having a one-size-fits-all approach.

In fact, sticking with the car analogy just a bit longer, if we tried to give Sarah a BMW, the cost of a single repair might bankrupt her, just as some medical procedures might. A healthcare equivalent of this might be a person with limited economic, transportation, and time-off-from-work degrees of freedom seeking care on location at the legendary Mayo Clinic. We not only must operate within the realities of the health benefit segments we've discussed, but there are also legitimate constraints, such as geographical and cost realities, that are inherent in the healthcare ecosystems each of us inhabit. We may not like it, but a rural consumer in an economically depressed part of the country that is facing doctor shortages and clinic closings either has to go elsewhere for healthcare if they are to benefit from the widest range of health resources and technologies or find virtual ways to access that care. Not everything for such a consumer can be fixed by the use of telemedicine, but if such simple technology allows our rural consumer and his or her healthcare provider to consult with a renowned specialist or reduce the number of trips to a regional medical center, they've come a lot closer to placing BMW performance inside an affordable sedan. Like a Kia, quality demands thoughtful value engineering.

Clinicians Need Benefits and SDoH Information to Optimize Health

Doctors don't often go through medical school to become experts at understanding healthcare insurance benefits or social science. In fact, benefit plans and reimbursement details are a great source of irritation and burnout for physicians. Nonetheless, whether you are speaking with individual physicians or hospital board members, I have little doubt that they are being compassionately sincere when, as over the years I have repeatedly heard them do, they say things like "We're going to treat all patients with the same standard of care whether they're a Medicare patient, a Medicaid patient, or a commercial patient." Because they are intelligent, I also have little doubt that they quickly learn that their reimbursement model is different for each of those segments. Physicians have a remarkable knowledge base and hard-earned skills, but they are still people, with constraints on their time and economic pressures to find their way within the complexity of an often-siloed healthcare system. And because people are people, they, like the vast majority of us, are guilty of making some generalized assumptions about strangers based on observable factors. That may not be the result of inherent bias as much as being able to apply heuristics and logical skills of deduction. But when I hear medical professionals and administrators nobly say things like they will provide the same standard of care no matter what benefit segment the person in question fits into, I challenge them—not because I doubt their genuine desire to treat all patients equally, but for a different reason. My response is "If you treat them exactly the same in terms of your processes with them, then you're failing them. If you don't at least know the benefit plan type of the patient in front of you and some basic SDoH data, then you're not going to be the best doctor you can be." In fact, I encourage providers and provider organizations to develop differentiated workflows based on benefit types and think of commercial, Medicare, and Medicaid as lines of business. In the US healthcare system, unless we anchor our innovation into the starting point of the benefit plan type, we are deceiving ourselves about our ability to create a personalized set of health improvement resources that can be applied with any practicality.

I make these challenges to my industry colleagues who deliver healthcare services because of some important realities. If the patient that a physician is treating has no way to afford the medication prescribed, can't reasonably read the prescription label instructions, can't attend business hour appointments because they have a manager who refuses to grant them time off, or has no one to watch their children in order to schedule and complete a lab procedure, that doctor can't really care for that patient in the same manner they could someone who does not face similar constraints. By doctors understanding the underlying economics and relevant social determinants when face to face with a patient, they can certainly improve the systematic ways in which they render effective care to provide the best outcomes. To be clear, doctors, nurses, and administrators all understand this, but with all the magnificent efforts to turn out digital platforms to support the delivery and reimbursement of sickcare, benefits and SDoH information has not "hit the screen" yet in a reliable fashion. And doctors cannot become expert at the thousands of external resources—from apps to local social support programs—much less "prescribe" these resources. There are current efforts by the American Medical Association and others to figure out how to efficiently put such information in front of clinicians and some innovative companies that are attempting to automate the ability of clinicians to recommend and order holistic resources.[18] But such efforts are nascent.

There is good news on the horizon, I believe. For just as AI can be used to support clinicians on diagnosis and treatment, it can also be used to quickly distill the relationships of data about benefits, daily living, and SDoH so that it provides dramatic leverage that enables physicians to be much more informed regarding their patients. But keep in mind this thought: If AI allows for the distillation of expertise to be quickly applied to patients, how are we going to integrate something the industry has never done at scale—moving from sickcare to optimized health for all healthcare consumers?

CHAPTER 4

CONSUMERS ARE SOMETIMES PATIENTS BUT ALWAYS CONSUMERS

I ended the last chapter quite consciously using the term "patients" as I referenced physicians and hospital board members speaking about the individuals for whom they provide care, and I used the term "consumers" as I reinforced the reality that any meaningful change will necessarily pivot off of existing segmented benefits systems, who often use the term "member." One of my pet peeves is that many people who work in the healthcare industry often use hyphenated descriptions like "member-patient" or "patient-consumer." They do so to be politically correct and, frankly, because they are confused. Speaking as a person with a chronic condition who has run the gamut of patient and member experiences on the one hand and been an executive for health plans, health services, and large employers on the other,

> *When it comes to the healthcare system, you are sometimes a patient and always a consumer.*

I have had good reason to spend many years sorting out the terminology. To simplify—when it comes to the healthcare system, you are sometimes a patient and always a consumer.

What's the Difference between a Patient and a Consumer?

The sickcare system is built to treat people as patients. An optimized health system would view people as consumers.

The picture below illustrates some key concepts:

Patient Claims & Clinical Data

- Diagnosis Codes
- Health Conditions
- Medications
- Procedure History
- Genomics
- And more ...

Consumer Daily Living Data

- Benefit Plan Type
- Household Composition
- Credit/Debt Information
- Online Presence
- Purchasing Habits
- Commuting Patterns
- Wealth Status
- Ethnicity
- Education
- And other SDoHs

A *patient* receives care from clinicians. A *consumer* makes choices in their clinical care and their daily living. When physicians use the term "patient engagement," they are generally referring to whether the individual is compliant as it relates to scheduling and follow-up and adherent to taking their prescribed medications. When I use the term "consumer engagement," this is something quite different, although complementary to patient engagement. In healthcare, "engaged consumers" are accountable for their overall health status and for the cost of achieving that status across a range of activities. In other words, they are vital participants in both denominator components of the unifying equation to produce the highest healthcare value.

If sickcare is reactive, health optimization is proactive.

If sickcare is *reactive*, health optimization is *proactive*. Moreover, while a patient-centric view focuses value on reimbursing providers for treating illness, a consumer-focused vision emphasizes identifiable benefits for individuals when they take action that improves their health status. With an optimized healthcare approach, consumers are empowered to make decisions and pursue healthy lifestyle choices. They are provided resources that further their personalized health education and inform them about the economics of their actions and choices. They are also connected to a personalized ecosystem of health improvement resources that includes, but goes well beyond, clinical resources. Optimized health is consumer driven because its goal is to promote a person's highest possible health status, ideally doing so with enough success to maintain a flatter morbidity curve longer. After all, if biology allows us to reach our optimal health in our twenties, shouldn't we approach healthcare in a way that does its best to extend that healthy status for as long as possible?

Let's return to holistic thinking about consumers versus patients and consider how Fred's needs are not addressed solely by the clinical care he receives. He needs social interaction and support more than ever because his wife is no longer the social director of his life. He would benefit from counseling to address the guilt he feels in his new position as caregiver because every minute he doesn't spend trying to help his wife, he feels like he's doing something less than he should. He needs connections to relevant educational materials that he can easily consume, to others who are experiencing serving in similar caregiving capacities, and to experts who can provide proven advice. Curated easy access to such programming would be but a start toward optimized health and well-being for Fred. Like Fred's newfound status as someone living on a fixed income and encountering an unfamiliar role as a caregiver, we all experience changes in our lives that are unplanned or unwanted. Some of these changes are more impacted by social determinants, and some are more driven by physical health issues. However and whenever these circumstances occur, we all make choices about how we lead our lives, and we have responsibility as consumers to be accountable for taking care of ourselves and our families the best that we can.

In my own case, despite being diagnosed with a chronic disease at age nineteen and being pummeled with seven major surgeries and all sorts of unpleasant complications that affect me each and every day, I maintain strict fitness, nutritional, and social regimens that I have developed and modified over more than thirty years. That's me being an engaged healthcare consumer as part of accomplishing optimal health while living daily with the physical health realities of Crohn's disease. I consciously recognize the social determinant impacts that surround me and support me in fulfilling my purpose as an executive leader, as a partner, as a parent, and most recently as a grandparent. I am keenly aware that other people face difficult challenges and of the Yiddish proverb that roughly translates into "Man plans, and God laughs." So, despite my intensive efforts to hold things together, I am extremely grateful for the fact that I have a great family and a supportive spouse, that I am in a position of no significant financial stress, that my attendance at religious services provides me spiritual health, and my participation as a volunteer and as a leader in my community offers me satisfaction in purpose and the pleasure of helping others. I am certain that if I didn't have—and consciously cultivate—these positively impactful social determinants in my life, my physical health condition would be worse, possibly debilitating, and I would probably become an archetype of a person with a serious and expensive set of chronic illnesses with accompanying mental health challenges, such as depression.

What are the equivalent holistic needs specific to Fred, María, Sarah, Sam, or any other individual? The point about my own daily living circumstances as impacted by my current social determinants—positive impacts of family and friends, finances, purposeful involvement in my community—is central to pursuing the daily living component of the equation in the case of my own health optimization. It also points to a broader point about health optimization generally. We cannot realize optimal health for any individual without understanding the personalized, interconnected elements of their life outside the traditional view of the sickcare system. We know that health status in the numerator of the equation is derived from choices we make and how we apply our time in the daily living part of the denominator. Accordingly, we must thoughtfully assess the ways in which SDoH factors impact choices and time that an individual is able to "invest" in creating or building productive, fulfilling personal and professional relationships, planning their financial future, staying mentally resilient, and operating within a value system that reinforces their self-purpose.

Contrast this holistically minded view of a consumer as presented in our equation's denominator with that of a clinical setting where you are identified by your condition. In hospitals, doctor's offices, and physical therapy clinics, you are a patient. Patients receive care. As I suggested at the beginning of this chapter, clinicians view engaged patients as compliant patients. Is the patient "complying" by taking their meds in accordance with the instructions or attending physical therapy? Of course, patient compliance is vital to achieving your best health status. Following our physician's orders can literally mean life or death. Consider a common example. Sarah is a type 2 diabetic. If she fails to monitor her blood glucose and properly manage her insulin levels, she's going to get really sick. She could get so sick that she enters a diabetic coma. Good doctors take care to guide their patients on the actions that can improve their conditions. But in seeing them only as patients, they tend to *define* them by their conditions. Having a good bedside manner, even when entirely sincere, is still different than knowing a patient as a person. And in order to achieve the kinds of personalized outcomes we discussed at the end of the last chapter and place people's best interests first, consumers need help. It's difficult to really help someone if you don't know them and their circumstances.

Consumers Take Actions and Make Choices

There is something even more important underlying this distinction of patients versus consumers. If patients are largely viewed by whether or not they are compliant, and if they are viewed as the recipients of "treatments" or the receivers of prescribed medications, they become the objects rather than the subjects of verbs; they become those to whom clinicians do things—procedures, lab tests, and so on. Consumers, in contrast to patients, make choices and take actions.

> *Consumers, in contrast to patients, make choices and take actions.*

Because Sarah has diabetes, she needs to actively follow strict daily protocols to stay healthy, including informed dietary choices to maintain that health—choices her primary physician has very little time or ability to help her make. Sarah lives in a decaying urban center, an old urban apartment-style neighborhood squeezed between gleaming office towers and a failing industrial district. The closest grocery store requires a lengthy bus ride with questionable safety characteristics. Often her only practical option is to use the convenience stores that are within walking distance to procure food for her family. She lives in what we now label a food desert. Sarah's dietary choices are somewhat dictated by the lack of availability of fresh foods in her neighborhood and the relatively high cost of some of the food choices that are present that could provide her the most benefit. Every individual is different, of course, but are we wrong to assume that Sarah might make different nutritional choices if she had healthy food options conveniently available at a price she could realistically afford?

By comparison, Sam doesn't suffer from diabetes, or from any chronic condition. At least not yet. The choices Sam makes today might determine whether that remains the case in his future. But on the rare occasions Sam interacts with medical professionals in a clinical setting, he tends to do so in a suburban urgent care center that's close to his apartment. When he does seek out care in such a clinic, is he treated as a consumer making choices for his healthy longevity or as a patient in need of a quick repair? The very nature of an "urgent" care facility is to treat immediate problems quickly and then move on to the next patient. They are not settings that promote getting to know a consumer's needs or offering detailed health management.

Engaged patients, therefore, are compliant patients in a paternalistic system that defines their care and treats or "cures" them, whereas engaged consumers independently make choices and complete actions that will help them achieve or maintain their optimal health. To do so, they take a holistic view of their health and consider what might make them healthier. They pay attention to what might increase their health status, such as exercise, good nutrition, and regular sleep. They avoid risky behaviors like smoking or excessive drinking. They have informed ideas about what affects their health status, and they're actively involved with and accountable for the activities they undertake.

Just as consumers are active in decision-making about their health, they are acutely aware of the costs associated with maintaining their health. Patients wonder if they are covered for the cost of their prescriptions, whereas a consumer thinks about the cost of maintaining overall health status. We see this when consumers contemplate the cost of a physical gym membership or online fitness subscription, or when buying fresh food products versus purchasing fast-food meal deals. An engaged health consumer reads articles and watches videos about the things they put in their body and considers the impact of trade-off decisions on their finances and their preferred lifestyle choices. Sometimes, components of clinical care like prescriptions cross over into the realm of consumer choice, as in contemplating the cost of a name brand versus generic drug or finding discount mechanisms at one pharmacy versus another.

Choice can (and should) include planning your finances when your health insurance open enrollment period rolls around each year. Perhaps your financial picture has changed in the last year, and now you're worried about whether you can still pay the $3,000 required to meet your annual deductible. An engaged consumer would investigate the impact of lowering their deductible and increasing their monthly premium contribution. According to a 2018 report from the Federal Reserve Board, 40 percent of Americans don't have the ability to cover a $400 emergency expense without borrowing money or selling something.[19] And $400 wouldn't cover a third of a breast needle biopsy, even if you went to an in-network provider. In a world where it costs

$2,659 to remove a plastic doll's shoe from a child's nose, as Katy and Michael Branson discovered, such financial decisions are not only real; they can have impacts that last for years.[20]

When you encounter the realities of how few people have the ready means to pay for even comparatively minor medical procedures out-of-pocket, we're reminded again what the last chapter emphasized: Consumers in different benefit segments often bear little relationship to one another when it comes to their financial flexibility and their buying power. As a result, it makes little sense to approach them only as patients in the traditional sense. Even if the clinical treatment for a diagnosed condition were the same for two different people, the same can't necessarily be said if you want to optimize the total health status of each of them.

Expanding the Healthcare Consumer Wallet

The term *consumer wallet* may be new to you, as it is not widely used today in the healthcare industry. If you recall, in the introduction I mentioned how much I enjoyed accountants in conversations at cocktail parties because they tend to be fact based. The concept of the consumer wallet is keeping track of the amount of total input costs attributed to an individual in healthcare. In the traditional sickcare system, it's fairly straightforward to keep track of what a consumer spends for their premium, for their copay, for coinsurance, for deductibles and other things related to the cost of clinical care. It's also fairly easy to tack the portion of clinical care that is paid by the insurance company, government, or employer. But if 70 percent of what drives health is daily living, then shouldn't the consumer healthcare wallet include the cost of health improvement resources for daily living? This would include the cost of access to nutrition and fitness programs, as well as resources designed to improve social relationships, improve mental resiliency, and promote healthier habits like smoking cessation. In a more holistic system, as we just discussed, health improvement resources to support daily living are also part of the input costs. In addition, any incentives provided to the consumer for taking actions to improve their health are also part of the input costs.

Might Fred make different consumer choices if he were directed and incented toward the five lifestyle behaviors—not smoking, moderate to vigorous exercise for at least 150 minutes a week, consuming a brain-supporting diet, light to moderate alcohol consumption, engaging in cognitive exercises—that a 2019 study from a Rush University demonstrated can help hold off dementia?[21] This large-scale study presented at the 2019 Alzheimer's Conference, like others that have preceded it, demonstrates precisely why we need to be educating consumers and providing them ready access to lifestyle changes that can directly impact their health. Shouldn't the cost of Fred's access to such information and to experts that could help him realistically make health-based lifestyle changes be part of his healthcare consumer wallet?

Shouldn't the cost of Fred's access to such information and to experts that could help him realistically make health-based lifestyle changes be part of his healthcare consumer wallet?

We are quick to acknowledge that healthcare is a $3.5 trillion industry. This equates to about 22 percent of the gross national product.[22] But if we expand our vision of the healthcare consumer wallet, the reality is that those figures are likely twice as high. Slowly, we are beginning to recognize this fact. For example, Medicare is beginning to introduce programs that can solidify a person's recovery. When an elderly person leaves the hospital, they often live in environments where they have difficulty caring for themselves. Maybe they live alone. Most likely they can't afford a home healthcare provider or a personal chef, so Medicare now is beginning to introduce programs where, for a period of time following hospital discharge, nutritionally balanced meals are delivered to their home as part of their benefit. Consider how likely a nutritional diet, one without the physical danger, difficult labor, and stress of cooking, can aid recovery and prevent a recurrent hospitalization.

Staying in the realm of Medicare, let's think about Fred again. Fred knows he gets dizzy sometimes. He knows that just getting around feels more difficult all the time and that he sometimes loses his balance. But because he's likely to get seven to fifteen minutes with his doctor when he sees him and his doctor has a lot to cover just reviewing Fred's recent test results and current medications, he's not likely to have time to discuss the complex topic of fall prevention. Yet a fall can be a major health setback for an elderly person. It may kill someone like Fred. Yet is Fred's doctor going to talk about proper walking aids or review his eyeglass prescription? Is he going to follow the CDC's "Stopping Elderly Accidents, Deaths, and Injuries Initiative" (STEADI) guidelines?[23] And if he were to follow those guidelines, how likely is he to help Fred enroll in a tai chi class, a proven way to greatly improve balance in the elderly?[24] Is he going to know Fred well enough to recognize that there's a class right in Fred's building that he could attend for free? Does he even know where Fred lives? Shouldn't fall-prevention aids be part of Fred's consumer wallet?

When we think about Sarah, our Medicaid recipient, what kind of total savings and elevated health status could be realized if she had resources to escape her food desert? Such a question offers an entirely different point that has rarely been considered in the sickcare benefits system. Yet if we can help Sarah achieve balanced nutrition for herself and her family, the impact to her total health will be every bit as substantial as any clinical intervention might be. Indeed, since she is a type 2 diabetic, proper nutrition is a critical element to her disease management.

The illustration below shows the significant difference between thinking about the consumer wallet in traditional clinical care terms and the types of resources that should surround a consumer in order to achieve health optimization.

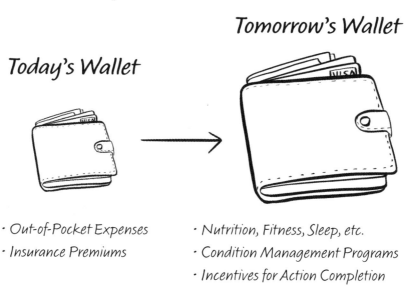

Today's Wallet
- Out-of-Pocket Expenses
- Insurance Premiums

Tomorrow's Wallet
- Nutrition, Fitness, Sleep, etc.
- Condition Management Programs
- Incentives for Action Completion

Targeting and Tracking Consumer Actions to Optimize Health

Let's think more about targeting people with the right personalized resources in healthcare by examining nonhealthcare successes. To return to an analogy for a moment, I've already reminded you that there's not a lot of sense in trying to sell a BMW 7 series to someone for whom a Kia Rio might max out their budget or bankrupt them when a repair becomes necessary. But we also live in a world where, whether it's cars or something else, we're continuously assaulted by advertisements for things we think we want. Or we're told to want. That's not going to change. The only change is that there are more entities using more new approaches to tell us what we are supposed to want. Essentially, isn't that the ultimate reality of most social media platforms? It's probably not a stretch to say that traditional public service announcements are not as effective at altering people's behavior as is tech-enabled advertising. Most of the advertising we're familiar with for products that could affect our health, like highlighting healthier food options on the menu of a fast-food restaurant or appealing to you to take out a gym membership, are carefully targeted at you, but they're not done in your best interests. I hate to burst your bubble, but they just want your money. How do they try to appeal to you? That gym membership or diet program is going to present you with images of a lot of rock-hard bodies that probably aren't any more realistic for most people than purchasing a BMW 740i. When you buy that $2,200 exercise bike, not only do the classes not come with it but neither does that modern glass-walled apartment featured in their advertisements. The reality of getting people to take actions to improve their health is a lot harder than advertising. Health improvement is hard work, for it demands life change. The other reality is that ad tech has more rapidly changed behaviors in people's daily living than anything in the history of humankind.

The reality of getting people to take actions to improve their health is a lot harder than advertising. Health improvement is hard work, for it demands life change.

I'm not looking to take on the ad tech industry. Nor am I of the belief that we can combat the effects of a culture where so much content we see daily is determined by social influencers and marketers. We're still going to click the "like" button, follow the images of the people and products we like, and frequently make consumer choices to buy products we won't use frequently or that we can't quite afford. Advertising, and the social effects it can produce, is too central to our economy. Instead, when thinking about how to get better health choices in front of consumers, we're probably much better off taking an "if we can't beat them, join them" approach.

One of the things Google, Facebook, Amazon, and others can teach us is that we live in times where targeting specific consumers has become extraordinarily effective. Yep, those shoes you looked at online two weeks ago are still showing up in your feed—within your email, your social media, and the games you play on your phone. If we can take some of this powerful ability to target individuals but do so in a way that actually caters to their best interests, we can provide them a real ability to make useful choices. What happens when instead of constantly selling people things they don't need, we connect them to the resources that can make their lives better? More importantly still, aren't you more likely to take advantage of those resources when they've been tailored specifically to *your* health needs and take into account *your* daily living and your healthcare benefits?

Consumers don't want to and can't do it alone. In the same way that Netflix serves up relevant content and personalized recommendations, healthcare can too. We have learned that by using information technology in a systematic approach, we can tie information campaigns to a person's physician or health plan or other entity that is relevant directly to them. In the same way advertising can affect the behavior of a consumer to make purchases, we can affect the behavior of a consumer to take action. We live in an age in which we can personalize health and well-being recommendations. The more relevant and personalized the messaging is to a consumer in terms of showing that you understand who they are, what their situation is, and what they're concerned about, the more likely they are to take those actions that can improve their health status.

Another lesson we can take from our deeply integrated digital economy is that, much like loyalty programs that might cause you to use the same airline or stay in the same hotel, if you attach an incentive to the completion of an action, it's more likely to get done. This is one of those "duh" moments about people being people. "You mean that if I buy nine macchiatos, you'll give me a tenth one free?" "If I upgrade my burrito to a meal and I come back tomorrow, I'll get ten percent off?" Duh! If we can incentivize consumers to take actions that benefit their health, they are far more likely to do so. The health improvement Sarah can experience from building meals around fresh fruits and vegetables may be intangible to her. If she can purchase fruits and vegetables at a reduced cost, she's incented to make the choice. By making the choice to change her diet, she receives a value-based benefit.

There are many ways to use economics to promote positive action. Incentivized rewards, waivers of payments, waivers of copay premiums, and gaming techniques for group and individual challenges can be mechanisms to reward consumers for using their benefits in ways that make them healthier. The important point here is that even by providing a richer set of total health improvement resources, the need for accessing the extraordinarily high costs of sickcare can be reduced. Such a system not only can save the consumer money but doing so can also directly and indirectly reduce the total healthcare spend.

In order to practically achieve an expansion of this holistic set of health improvement resources and incentives to expand the consumer wallet, we need a new type of transaction in healthcare—I call it the *consumer action transaction.* I have written elsewhere about typical shopping or purchase transactions we undertake almost daily, whether online or at a cash register. In the clinical care world, when a physician or other medical professional performs a service on a patient, the resulting transaction is called a "claim" or an "encounter." This establishes that the service occurred and what the charge is. But when a consumer does something that affects their health, either for better or for worse, that action is not, in today's world, recorded as a transaction. The action could be walking, eating the right or the wrong food, staying hydrated, participating in a coaching session about substance abuse, viewing information on their health benefits, doing a health risk assessment, self-checking their blood sugar level, or any number of things one can do as a consumer. Because we developed benefits for sickcare, the procedural and technology systems in place today allow for the collection of data regarding professional services performed relating to an individual or a population fairly easily. By contrast, the healthcare industry has not uniformly implemented processes and information technology to categorize, track, or aggregate consumer actions. This makes it impossible to relate the cause and effect of consumer actions to health status, the numerator of our unifying equation.

If you have a choice of affecting the behavior of 550,000 physicians through value-based reimbursement or 325 million American consumers through value-based benefits, which do you think is more powerful?

If you can't track consumer actions that affect health in daily living, then you can't measure value obtained from those actions. Since daily living impacts 70 percent of our health, the lack of such a systems approach makes it difficult to improve healthcare value consistently. Yet there are ways to aggregate such actions. How to do so is one part of a systematic approach we'll discuss in the next chapter. Building a systematic framework for how consumers can encounter and access the things that provide them choice is also a central part of what we'll discuss next.

Let's conclude this chapter with a big thought about enabling people to become healthcare consumers versus patients who have things done to them. If you have a choice of affecting the behavior of 550,000 physicians through value-based reimbursement or 325 million American consumers through value-based benefits, which do you think is more powerful?

When we treat people as consumers and provide them the power of choice, we open up opportunities for them to assume greater responsibility for their health. Shouldn't that be a goal of healthcare?

Part III: To Love and to Cherish

Providing Consumers Tools for Total Well-Being

CHAPTER 5

SCALING EXPERTISE TO PERSONALIZE A YEAR-IN-THE-LIFE FOR CONSUMERS

I've already spent a fair amount of time drawing analogies from the convenience of living in an age when we are able to shop from our home computers or mobile devices. With the touch of a button, our product choice is purchased and on its way to our doorstep. We are repeatedly told, by both mass media and trade media, that the companies that sell to us online use AI to "know what we need before we ask." While this omniscient AI might be exaggerated, how can this thought process from the world of digital retail apply to getting each of us health improvement resources in our daily living?

To think about the journey from digital retail purchasing to healthcare daily living, let's consider another kind of consumer product purchase experience for a moment, one that is not yet primarily accomplished online. I hope you, like me, have had the experience of shopping in a small local hardware store that features an owner who possesses a seemingly limitless supply of knowledge. He's the kind of expert who can walk you down an aisle, immediately find you the part or tool that is going to solve your quandary, and even tell you exactly how to complete the project that got you out of bed on a Saturday before you had your second cup of coffee. The guy's such a repository of knowledge there hardly seems a question that can stump him. And because he provides you with personal attention, you feel confident you will walk out of his store with precisely what you need. You exit with your tools, supplies, and advice, newly confident in your ability to execute your task or project.

The next time you're in need, you'll just go directly to that same expert owner, right? After all, past trips have shown you that even his best employees don't exactly match his knowledge base. With them it's more of a hit-and-miss affair, and you spend a lot more time searching for a part or tools you can't name. And that's exactly my point. You've experienced this great resource, but it's impossible to consistently scale. If there were ten other customers in the store at the same time you were there, he certainly couldn't have helped them all at the same time or with the same amount of personalized focus.

Imagine scaling that problem over tens of millions of people. Impossible, right? Big-box home improvement stores—unless you are skilled in finding what you need—are, well, big. And despite a plethora of YouTube "how-to" videos, the online experience isn't the same as information tailored just for you. Moreover, zeroing in on the exact parts (and supporting tools) you need for your home repair, while likely available, isn't exactly an online retailer's strong suit.

You won't be surprised that expertise on your total health and well-being isn't the strong suit of most of the tech giants either, no matter how many companies they buy or supply. The online retail universe is interested in selling you things that you may or may not need. Such online marketplaces are experts at building you recommendation lists on things you're likely to buy but don't care what you do with them once you've hit the "buy now" button. And YouTube, well, it can be a rich repository of information—or misinformation—based on the search you embark on and the source you select. But the maker of the YouTube video bears no accountability for incomplete or errant advice. If only, as it relates to your total health, you could combine the hardware store owner's knowledge base and his personalized attention and scale it digitally to the level of Amazon or YouTube.

Here's the question for our purposes: How do you weave together the richest possible tapestry of health improvement resources available, specific to a person's individual needs? Unless we suddenly master human cloning and replicate the healthcare superstar equivalent of Mr. Hardware Store a few million times, we've got to build a systematic framework. And we then have to scale that framework using digital information technology. As we learned in chapter 3, any framework has to start with recognizing the role of health benefits, or we won't understand the system's constraints. In my experience, the best solutions to solving a problem are established when you understand the constraints of a system and optimize within that system, and we now have some grounding in the major types of benefits that consumers have. Starting, then, at the means of access an individual has to the system through their health benefits, we can use the power of personalized data available through digital information technology to weave this tapestry.

A Tapestry of What

Before we step over to our digital loom or even try to imagine what might comprise our total health and well-being tapestry, let's be very clear that we are now talking about how to solve the scaling of health improvement resources for our daily living, not for clinical care. Let's look again at the denominator of the equation.

$$H_v = \frac{\textit{Health Status (person or population)}}{\textit{Clinical Care ("omics") + Daily Living (SDoH)}}$$

Because of contemporary headline news topics, I am compelled to comment briefly on applying digital technology as it relates to clinical care. It's easy to jump to the conclusion that telemedicine is the digital equivalent of online retail for clinical care that can always provide lower-cost clinical care in the denominator. But that is often not the case because there is a service delivery component involved as opposed to just goods, and online visits are not necessarily less expensive. During a televisit the actual value received is conveyed during the time of the online interaction, which is not digitally scalable. In other words, there is still one-to-one interaction between the clinician and the patient for as much time as it takes, one at a time, just like waiting for the hardware store expert to become available. Don't misunderstand my point, as I am a huge supporter of this form of virtual clinical care for many circumstances. The site-alternative convenience value of virtual visits was brought front and center throughout the COVID-19 crisis of 2020, and there will be many opportunities to use remote monitoring and applied AI in the future to scale clinical assistance with more digital technology and less expert human capital. Expect to see much more of both telemedicine and remote monitoring in a combined system of virtual and physical delivery.

Going back to scalability of resources to support daily living, there's a lot to think about regarding how we inject expertise in a systematic way to create healthcare that would mimic the expertise, personalization, and localization of the hardware store owner in a practical way. We often hear the phrase that a business is there to "serve their community." In healthcare lingo the concept of a community can also be described as "the population we serve." But here's the rub: You can't manage and serve a population in healthcare (or anything else) unless you can first effectively serve an individual. The health status or underlying healthcare costs of a population is built one person at a time, which is why I spent a chapter focused on personalization and the importance of viewing people as consumers rather than patients.

> *You can't manage and serve a population in healthcare (or anything else) unless you can first effectively serve an individual.*

Finishing up the hardware analogy, we have all heard the phrase "When you have a hammer, everything looks like a nail." But in truth, what we love about our hardware store hero is that they thoughtfully consider and solve the problem. They discern whether the issue at hand is creating something new, maintaining something that's working, fixing something that's broken, or doing something else. And they also talk through the whole problem, considering whether it's better to fix or replace based on your budget, or whether you have most of the tools and supplies you need, or need just one or two key items. They remember or have a record of the brand of power tool you bought previously, and they ensure the exact right part.

We all desire to have a problem solved in our context, and not to be sold to based upon a narrow perspective of a singular skill set or product offering. When the current institutional players in the healthcare industry focus on the whole person and provide resources to a consumer based upon the problem the consumer is trying to solve, magical things can happen. Conversely, when a health plan, employer, or provider thinks about their own goals without sufficient consideration for what the consumer is trying to accomplish, well, we all know what that feels like. If a health plan's goal is to manage utilization against premiums to increase profitability, as consumers we feel that as a lack of provider choice or inhibited access in obtaining care. If a provider is trying to get better utilization of its equipment and facilities to be able to garner additional revenue, we feel it as unnecessary tests and procedures—even though no harm has been done. And if an employer is trying to lower medical claims costs for higher-risk employees, we might be asked to enroll in a condition management program that may or may not be a good fit for our circumstance.

As we'll see in chapter 7, there is a systematic way to accomplish combined goals for healthcare entities and consumers through consumer activation. But before we get to that, we need to step back and think more about the reality of a consumer living their 99 percent daily living life and coming into contact with their 1 percent clinical life. About a decade ago, I had the opportunity to sit down with senior executives from every type of healthcare incumbent organization and work with them to deconstruct a generalized consumer taxonomy for healthcare. The truth is that when most healthcare organizations sit down to map and improve what they usually refer to as a "consumer journey," they are actually thinking about when their entity comes into contact with a consumer and how to make that "better" to accomplish their own goals. Far less frequently they start with a blank piece of paper and put themselves into the shoes of a consumer. But just like our local hardware store owner, we would all do better to listen carefully to the problem before offering a solution.

A Year-in-the-Life

But what's the "right perspective" from the consumer point of view? When I discuss a framework that works for a consumer's approach to healthcare, I refer to a principle I call a "year-in-the-life." This taxonomy represents the thinking of highly seasoned healthcare executives, as well as patients and consumers, who are not constrained by solving for any one type of healthcare entity. That being said, my framework on year-in-the-life is absolutely biased by my conviction that in the US healthcare system—or any other system—the type of benefit plan is the foundation for how we think through the constraints of providing the best health improvement resources at the lowest total cost. And even though healthcare doesn't occur based on a calendar year, benefit plans most often do. On the following page is a graphical representation of the basic components of a year-in-the-life.

Each of these categories has numerous subcategories, but for the purposes of this book, we'll stay high level. The important point here is not to necessarily think about a calendar year but the systematic things that happen across the year-in-the-life of a healthcare consumer.

Understanding Your Risks and Needs

The first step in the year-in-the-life of a consumer is to understand your health risks and needs. All the benefit types we've discussed, whether private or government-run, have the equivalent of an open enrollment period or a set of standards that determine your eligibility to obtain coverage. In order to get yourself and your family into the best situation, you want to spend

If we take healthcare personalization seriously, then we first must acknowledge that our health is always in flux.

YEAR-IN-THE-LIFE

UNDERSTAND MY RISKS AND NEEDS	MAXIMIZE VALUE OF MY BENEFITS	MANAGE AND IMPROVE MY HEALTH	GET HEALTH AND WELLNESS SERVICES	GET HEALTH AND WELLNESS GOODS	SEEK INFORMATION AND SUPPORT
✓ Understand my overall health status and risk factors	✓ Determine my sources of healthcare funding	✓ Participate in healthy behaviors and activities	✓ Actively monitor and address behavioral issues impacting my health and wellness	✓ Meet my nutritional needs	✓ Efficiently locate and access health information that is personalized to me
✓ Understand my health budget and risk tolerance	✓ Understand how my actions impact my costs—including reward systems	✓ Optimize my controllable health factors	✓ Monitor my health and select highest value settings to obtain ongoing care	✓ Maintain my required medical supplies	✓ Securely and privately engage in health conversations with people "like me"
✓ Assess my requirements for consumer-based degrees of freedom	✓ Select my benefits plan and understand my financial obligations	✓ Utilize biometric monitoring, and triage services to reduce episodes and financial exposure	✓ Triage my care using consumer support tools and my population health partner(s)	✓ Fill my prescriptions and take them compliantly	✓ Get rewarded for "doing my homework"
	✓ Determine my population health management partner(s)	✓ Manage my known health challenges	✓ Follow my care plan	✓ Consider applicability of breakthrough science innovations to my health circumstances and economics	✓ Seek environments that support the management and optimization of my health, and my family's health
			✓ Schedule and obtain care in an appropriate care setting (physical or virtual)		

some time thinking about your own current health and that of your family members. There are multiple types of resources available to assess your health and risk. Ironically, many of these assessments occur *after* you have enrolled in your benefits options. And as we already discussed, nearly everybody is herded into a particular benefits segment based on some combination of age, employment status, and economic status.

What I am emphasizing here is that we need to find better ways to put information tools and analytics into the hands of consumers before they make decisions about their benefit options. In a personalized way, they become engaged in anticipating what your healthcare needs are likely to be over the next year or so. Such prescience is demanding, for if we take healthcare personalization seriously, then we first must acknowledge that our health is always in flux. You simply are not the same person you were a year ago. Not only have you aged, but perhaps your diet has also changed or you have suffered a health episode, developed a new chronic condition, or had an accident or injury. But we still must start each benefit year with this question: What's your health status *today*?

There is another key question that should be asked before you get to benefits enrollment: What are your economic, transportation, and scheduling degrees of freedom for variations over the next year? While some of these questions are at the heart of SDoH, let's uncomplicate it for a moment. Can you afford a cost surprise of more than $500? Do you have the mobility to safely access care that isn't very close to where you live? Do you work in a job that is jeopardized if you can't adhere to a rigid set of hours? One of the reasons we heard about lower-wage workers getting adequate sick leave during the COVID-19 crisis was because that accommodation was certainly not a standard.

NOT JUST IN SICKNESS ... BUT ALSO IN HEALTH

There are many health assessment and predictive analytic resources that could greatly improve the ability of individual consumers to do their best possible planning on their own behalf and on behalf of their families. In general, you may know that most benefit plans encourage an annual wellness check with your primary provider. Wouldn't it make common sense to also assess your health status at the end of your benefits year and *before* you determine what plan you are going to enroll in for the upcoming period? In other words, to the extent possible, think about proactively budgeting for your health.

To conclude the topic of understanding your risks and needs, let me remind you that when you assess your health, you should not only think about your physical health, which is often easier to think about (e.g., chronic condition, acute injury, need for surgical or dental procedure, etc.) but also your mental health, your relationship status and support systems you have in place, and, of course, your financial health. In chapter 7 I'll discuss ways the government, health plans, employers, and providers can systematically connect you to the right resources to solve your personal situation. So, as you can see, the question "What's your health status today?" is far more complicated than the biological health of your body. But it is a question that can be solved.

Maximize the Value of Your Health Benefits

Hopefully, by the time you enroll in your health benefits plan you have assessed your risks and needs so you know what you want to get out of the plan to best create value for you in your situation. Even if you have not, when your benefits eligibility starts, you should be thinking about how you derive the most *value* from your health insurance premiums or payments to providers, remembering that achieving and maintaining your highest health status at the lowest cost is the goal.

As I said earlier, the segmentation and standardization of benefits types is quite helpful here. Because health benefits are largely regulated, you can actually get answers to benefits questions, although the complexity of benefits often requires the use of AI assistance to get the right answers. In simple terms, however, you are asking this: What sort of access do you have to healthcare based on your benefit plan? Can you get the treatment you need? Who will pay for it? How much will treatment cost you? Do you have a high-deductible plan? Have you put enough money in a health savings account to cover the deductible that is your responsibility? And, one of my favorites, what incentives and rewards are you eligible to receive if you engage in recommended actions designed to improve your health? Such questions illustrate a logical step two of the year-in-the-life approach. You are quite literally trying to ensure that you get what you deserve in terms of maintaining and improving your health or, as I have labeled it, "maximize the value of your benefits."

Let's check in on our four illustrative individuals. Just as María's health is different from Fred's, their benefit plans are different. María's commercial health plan may provide what seems like a set of BMW 7 Series options and rich financial incentives for participating in wellness programs. By contrast, Fred's Medicare plan may feel like choosing from options on a midpriced domestic sedan, enough to reliably get him from place to place, and if he takes the right actions, maybe he gets the equivalent of a free tank of gas. In actuality, Fred may easily have the financial means to access the same resources as María at a lower cost, but doing so would take him outside his managed Medicare network. But Fred, like many of his fellow seniors, may be reluctant to incur out-of-pocket expenses even if he is financially able to because he loves his "zero premium plan." Sam is hindered regarding his year-in-the-life because he's terrible at assessing his risks and needs while simultaneously unlikely to feel he has many constraints. As a result, Sam, if he uses healthcare resources to any extent, may not choose the ones that can benefit him most to proactively manage his health. And Sarah—well, Sarah presents an interesting case. She may actually possess access to the richest set of benefits through Medicaid, if only she knew what they were and how they applied to her. I'll come back around to Sarah before this chapter is over, for she's revealing of how health optimization can be transformative.

Manage Your Own Care

The third category of a year-in-the-life is managing your own care. Nearly everyone understands that if they get a cold or the flu, there's a lot they can do to make themselves better—getting rest, increasing fluid intake, and taking over-the-counter medicines. These are healthcare needs that generally don't require the intervention of a health professional.

Such self-care is fundamental to daily living, as is living a healthy lifestyle—trying to provide balanced meals for you and your family and watching your own weight through nutrition and exercise, undergoing smoking cessation programs, or ensuring that you don't abuse alcohol and steering clear of other habit-forming compounds. We have plenty of evidence that people benefit from programmatic help on these issues. Generally, we hold a presumption that despite the ready availability of dangerous substances or unhealthy food options, people have some ability to manage their consumption. People are different, and the social determinants that impact them are different. Of course, knowing what's right and doing what's right are two different things, but every action an individual takes has an overt impact on their health.

The next part of managing your own care in daily living is managing any diagnosed medical condition. Condition management is something that, for the most part, a person can do without any significant amount of intervention by a clinician. Just as more and more options are available to help people with fitness, nutrition, stress management, and other parts of their normal daily lives, health improvement resources that can help those with diagnosed medical conditions monitor and manage daily living are also becoming more prevalent and easier to access through digital technology. Sarah, for example, as a type 2 diabetic, must maintain a daily regimen of blood sugar and insulin control and would benefit from any number of resources, including education, help with supplies, and remote monitoring, that can aid her. Likewise, Fred can keep tabs on his borderline hypertension and Sam, if he chose, could monitor and manage his caloric and alcohol intake.

Get Professional Health Services

Now we get to the part of the sequence in a year-in-the-life that is something everybody understands—the need to access clinical care! No matter how much we self-manage, sometimes we simply need the help of healthcare professionals. As a nation, we spend a few trillion dollars on this each year.

It seems only common sense that we all should want to do whatever we are able to minimize hospitalizations, unnecessary trips to the emergency room or urgent care facilities, or the need for additional prescribed medications.

Of course, not all use of clinical care can, or should be, avoided. Quite the opposite. Health optimization practices and traditional clinical care should be a partnership, something we'll discuss more near the end of the book. And so, in the year-in-the-life of a consumer, we should expect at least a modicum of clinical interaction, whether we are lucky enough that such action is limited to annual wellness care visits to our primary physician and routine diagnostic tests or, when less lucky, involves seeking care because of an accident or injury, an illness, or treatment of an ongoing condition. The whole system has been set up to make sure there's lots of resources available in this arena of healthcare services, and the quality of that care can be excellent. We also need to think of professional healthcare services more expansively than traditional medical sickcare and dentistry. Systematically, healthcare services also include mental health, health coaching for conditions, social support, nutrition counseling, and perhaps exercise and fitness.

> *A promising evolution in clinical care is how we evolve from applying clinical expertise reactively toward prevention.*

A promising evolution in clinical care is how we evolve from applying clinical expertise reactively toward prevention. Think about Fred again; if his clinician notices that he has become unsteady and we can provide him with comprehensive programming on fall prevention, we may save him a lot of pain, stress, disablement, and expense. In the process we would help his wife by maintaining her companionship with her husband and allowing him continued participation in her care. And guess what? If Fred chooses to participate in these alternatives to keeping himself healthy, he will literally save you and me, taxpayers that we are, money.

Get Healthcare Goods

I have purposefully separated the professional health services above from healthcare goods. Going back to the hardware store analogy, part of what we appreciate is that we can present the problem, get the advice, and get all the supplies at once. But this one-stop convenience to solve a health problem, whether reactive or proactive, is not how healthcare generally works. In other words, in healthcare it is less common that you get your healthcare goods in the same place you get your advice. Whether we are talking prescription drugs, durable medical equipment like oxygen tanks and walkers, disposable goods like adult diapers or catheters, or over-the-counter medications, there's a huge array of medical goods available from both physical stores and via mail order. There is also a huge disconnect between the advice and the supplies, such that any combination of the complexity, cost, or inconvenience of a consumer chasing down supplies can cause otherwise sound (and expensive) advice to be wasted. Ironically, many of the items that healthcare consumers do not really need to improve their health are abundantly available and convenient. We can systematically do much better, as we will discuss later.

Seek Information and Support

Now, to bring all these aspects of a year-in-the-life approach together, we need one more vital thing: a foundation to get information, guidance, and support for any and all of the year-in-the-life categories I have discussed. The simple reality is that there are very few people who have expertise across all the categories. And those who are experts tend to specialize in only one of the categories. Think about our hardware store scenario. There are limited numbers of experts who gain proficiency in navigating people across all the categories to find the right services and supplies. Going back to an earlier point, you can't take care of a population unless you can take care of an individual person. Accordingly, no method of support can be effective without sufficient personalization that knows enough about a person to provide relevant information in each of the categories. That is why we need to know at least enough about each and every healthcare consumer to allow us to paint a more holistic picture, like we have of Sarah, Fred, María, and Sam.

To realize such a world, we need a systematic framework that harnesses the power of information technology. We need the power of AI and machine learning because even the most highly skilled person imaginable cannot consider all the combinations and permutations and get the right resources to the right people. And even if such a person existed, they could not be replicated to scale. Applied in both timely and correct ways, information technology can accomplish superheroic feats, but it requires the right approaches and the right minds to unleash its power.

How might our lives change if we had one common source of information support that was personalized? What improvements in Sarah's, Sam's, Fred's, and María's lives might take place if each of them had one place, individualized to their needs, to which they could turn to access the myriad resources available to them?

The next chapter offers answers to these questions and several more we haven't asked yet.

CHAPTER 6

DEFINING A SYSTEMATIC
FRAMEWORK THAT INCLUDES SDoH

What might a system that truly meets the needs of Sarah and Sam, María and Fred, and about 327 million (or 7 billion) other people look like? To start, let's revisit that equation from chapter 1 again.

$$H_v = \frac{\textit{Health Status (person or population)}}{\textit{Clinical Care ("omics")} + \textit{Daily Living (SDoH)}}$$

The equation takes us back to the concept of two-axis personalization. Recall from chapter 2 that one axis is personalized medicine, which equates to clinical care—the care provided by medical professionals. Recall also that "omics" is a multiplier to clinical care, as science will continuously get better at applying genomics, proteomics, metabolomics, and other "omics" to provide better ways to prevent and treat illness. By way of example, as someone who has Crohn's disease, I am keenly aware that through genetic research, scientists have discovered that good dietary advice for one individual may prove inappropriate or even harmful for another. Without "omics"—in this case, microbiomics—the use of nutrition to help manage my condition cannot be tailored to the unique needs of my biology and cellular makeup. And accordingly I look forward to the advancement of science that helps me and others with my disease achieve optimal clinical health. But as I am not a clinician, I simply do not possess the expertise to do justice to the intricacies and complexities of biological, biochemical, biophysical, or even bioethical sciences. Therefore, I will limit the scope of what I explain to the second axis: daily living. And, as we will see, social determinants are every bit as important a multiplier to daily living as "omics" are to clinical care.

Social Determinants in Daily Living

And what, again, is daily living? Well, it is that 99 percent (plus) part of your life lived outside of clinical care settings. It seems like discussion of our multiplier to daily living—social determinants—pops up today with frequency when people speak about the healthcare system, but nearly always as if it were a new epiphany. I was struck by how "surprised" people were during the early stages of the COVID-19 crisis that certain portions of our population got hit harder than others. This was no surprise to people paying attention to the uneven distribution of poverty and disease burden afflicting much of our minority population. In fact, the recognition about the importance of social determinants is not new at all. Think about the naming conventions in our governmental system at the federal level—the Department of Health *and Human Services*. Like its name implies, this cabinet-level agency administers programs that acknowledge the linkage between health *and* those things that are fundamental to a person's daily living. This linkage has long been recognized from a societal perspective, even if it is not adequately implemented across our society or is rarely reflected in the approaches taken in clinical care settings. Strengthening this linkage is what we have to address, and I am very excited regarding the opportunity to make a dramatic and positive difference.

So just what do I mean by understanding the multiplier effect of social determinants? One way to think about this is to focus on the environment we live in, including housing affordability, geography, recreational opportunities, access to transportation, and safety. A broader way to think about this is to examine whether a community is inclusive and supportive or whether it is a community prone to higher crime rates or has a higher percentage of citizens who are substance abusers. We all intellectually understand that places are different from one another and that those differences shape the lives of people who live in them. Places create identifiable localized cultures. A community that prides itself on being healthy is very different than one focused on industrial output or how good its sports teams are. This isn't a value judgment or a suggestion that one community is superior to another, but it is to say that an environment or "environmental culture" has broad repercussions on the lives people lead.

In addition to the environment we live in, we each have an individual set of certain personal social determinants that can be categorized. These include things like our level of education, our level of literacy in a given language, our level of fitness, and the mobility associated with it. Do we own a car? Do we take a bus or other form of public transportation? Do we work from within or outside our home? Of course, I recognize that disparities exist across racial and ethnic groups in the United States and around the world. But the best way to overcome these disparities is synonymous with how to achieve health optimization—that is, by knowing enough about an individual to provide them personalized resources in accordance with their situation. The systematic framework I am describing can solve social problems in the same way it can improve health, achieving better results at a lower cost.

Importantly, my use of the concept of personal social determinants also includes our stability, both in terms of financial wealth and primary and familial relationships. The latter measure of stability then extends outward to the relationships we have with friends and social groups. As with our families, these relationships may create personal networks that can be weak or strong, supportive or deleterious. A single mother like Sarah may have friends and family members who are stable, dependable, and supportive and thereby able to assist her regularly with childcare or help provide her family nutritious meals. Of course, Sarah could just as easily have friends and family members who are addicted to illegal substances, who participate in criminal activity, or who create negligent or abusive environments—what we collectively label "behavioral health concerns." If Sarah's primary relationships fall into this latter set of descriptors, even if those around her genuinely love and wish to help her, turning to them puts her and her children at risk.

There are dozens of additional social determinants we could identify, and we could spend significant time trying to categorize them, but doing so now is unimportant in comparison to understanding the profound multiplier effects they have on individual lives. Because María has a higher education level and a higher degree of literacy than Sarah, her ability to search for, interpret, and find appropriate health resources will generally be better than Sarah's. This is not a measurement of intelligence but rather one of opportunity and experience. Similarly, María's substantially higher income affords her the opportunity to

With changed circumstance comes changed need.

access available resources, to transport herself as needed to utilize those resources, to control her schedule, and to do it all safely. Because María is in a relationship with a stable and supportive spouse, she gains even greater advantage over Sarah.

I have repeatedly emphasized that a structured framework must be personalized. With changed circumstance comes changed need. Transform any key social determinant for these two women, and you will see why. Consider, for a moment, how different María's daily living would be if instead of having a supportive, stable husband, her husband is abusive. Not only is her day-to-day life entirely different, but her life needs also change, and her health is directly impacted. She may require regular clinical intervention because of injuries inflicted on her by her abuser, her mental health needs change entirely, her relationship with her children is affected, and the psychological effects of her abuse may in turn impact her nutrition or how she performs at work. Examine your own life or those of others you know, and you'll see how this ripple effect—negatively or positively—extends outward from one major life change. Obviously, the resources that might improve María's life and her health are entirely different with this one altered circumstance. Therefore, a set of personalized resources to support María would have to keep up with those changes.

The same would be true if Sarah had even one person in her life who had the flexibility and stability to become a source of reliable assistance. Give Sarah a grandmother, old enough to no longer work, young enough to still have good energy and mobility, and frugal enough over a lifetime to have a safe, stable home supplied with nutritious food. Additionally, give that grandmother a desire to support Sarah by providing her children a happy place to go after school each day, where they eat well, are made to feel safe, and receive encouragement to complete their homework—and Sarah's daily living is altered at myriad levels in a positive way.

What the above scenarios illustrate is that while the constraints of a benefits system guide initial access to resources, they don't necessarily paint a picture of the whole person. We could have a person with all the apparent privileges in the world battling a significant number of negative social determinants, and unless they can fight through these barriers to normalize their daily living, their total health and well-being is likely to get worse. This is true for the richest commercial benefit plan recipient, and it is just as true for seniors on Medicare or people in the Medicaid population.

The point I have just illustrated with these two women is exactly why we need a systematic framework for providing resources. It is absolutely possible that Sarah and María could "flip" places in terms of their total well-being starting points. As I have detailed, to create such a framework, we start at the types of benefits an individual has, we consider the reasons that an incumbent healthcare player might want to support the consumer or provide them outreach, and we consider what a consumer goes through in a year-in-the-life. Only then can we identify the right individualized health improvement resources useful for any person at the right time and in a way that those resources can be consumed.

Communicating and Interacting with Consumers in Daily Living

Because everyone is different, the communication methods and modalities to provide them access to effective resources must be tailored to individual needs. Sam, for example, lives on his smartphone. A mobile app is his best ticket to learn about a social group with whom he can share a weekend activity, to track his exercise, or to be reminded to moderate his alcohol intake. Fred's a hip grandpa and owns an iPhone. He's comfortable with his phone's features, but the small screen is difficult for him to read, so he prefers web-based resources he can access through his desktop computer with the bigger screen. María likes to talk directly to people, either face to face or on the phone—she won't even text her kids, much to their annoyance. What we know for certain is that digital-age technology allows us to target and deliver resources to consumers in ways that are the most effective they've ever been in the history of humankind. You may be annoyed at how items you have looked to purchase start to "follow you around" on the internet, showing up as pop-up ads. But that technology can also be extremely effective at teaching us how to get health resources to targeted individuals. We all have our preferences, whether those are brought to us digitally as apps, texts, chatbots, and online videos or in analog ways like in-person services, phone consultations, interactive voice exchange, smart speakers, or printed literature. We live in an age where the options for reaching consumers are wide open.

In fact, there are so many effective modalities to communicate with consumers about available resources that there is a real risk of them becoming overwhelmed. The downside of abundant consumer choice is confusion. How do you determine what approach to an exercise program is best for you when there are thousands of programs marketed at you? Which of them best fits your fitness level, your health conditions, your age, your experience, your medical needs? If you require assistance in managing your A1C, you are inundated with commercials offering competing products; which one is worth having a discussion with your doctor about? Is such a conversation even available to you?

Finding the right solution that will work for a person's daily living is not so simple. We could extend the exercise or A1C examples to every social determinant we can imagine. This abundance of resources, combined with the radical variation of individual needs, highlights why we need a systematic approach. You need to be able to classify and curate all the types of resources that might be available to a population and keep offerings comprehensive and current.

Let's go back to our magnificent hardware store owner. While he offers an incredible repository of knowledge, the store has to reflect how that knowledge and the products to which it is applied are classified and organized. Enter the store and you expect a logical arrangement of departments and aisles. You further expect signage and placement of products within those aisles that make items easy to identify and locate. You need bins and drawers that are clearly labeled with their contents. You need lumber identified by its type of wood and its dimension. And don't forget clear pricing! You expect the store to provide a vast array of goods and keep up with the latest products. Hardware, like everything else in the world, is constantly changing, improving, and becoming ever more specialized. Sound familiar?

With the Internet, creating a curated, ever-growing, ever-changing catalog is a whole lot easier than keeping up a physical hardware store. The big five tech firms—Google, Apple, Amazon, Microsoft, and Facebook—along with their smaller competitors, have proven that they are incredibly adept at teeing up a list of recommendations that appear to be tailored to our interests and "push" them to you. Online retailers can offer a catalog of things they have to sell, whether the items are in inventory or not. That is because they have also built a dynamic supply chain and rapid delivery capabilities. All of this ease of access, voluminous supply, and personalized buying recommendations does not necessarily mean they are working in the best interest of you, the consumer. Their ultimate interest is selling you more stuff. The algorithms they employ are sophisticated, and the amount of data they hold about you is massive. They're using a technique of surveillance that's based on activity you undertake online and then striking you in the right moment with the right enticing appeal. But at the end of the day, what they want to provide you is quite straightforward—a completed sale of items combined with a user experience that satisfies sufficiently so that you return to their platform for more transactions.

The mechanisms online retailers use to operate are not inherently bad. But when we use parts of the systematic approaches they employ to place health improvement resources before consumers, not only is the process a great deal more complicated, but the timely information and resources that a health plan, employer, provider, or other sponsoring organization is trying to inform consumers about are also provided to them precisely because they *are* in their best interests. This is not a sales campaign. If it is done right, you really are going to help optimize consumer health per our equation.

Optimizing health transforms lives. The focus cannot become a selling construct where we try to peddle more healthcare goods or services that the person may or may not need. Rather, it must be a focus on providing an accessible and efficient set of health improvement resources. Demand becomes less about what a consumer wants and more about what a consumer needs based on evidence-based constructs and on data we have about social determinants and drivers.

> *The focus cannot become a selling construct where we try to peddle more healthcare goods or services that the person may or may not need.*

In an age of AI and machine learning, matching such needs to an individual can and should be accomplished. All the data points about a person's daily living and social determinants, like the data about their clinical health, can be kept track of properly if there's an intent and a platform to do so. Believe me, it's not an easy thing to do, but it is possible. Unlike physical goods and services that need to be allocated across a population, virtual services in the form of knowledge, programming, education, and advice can be distributed at an unlimited rate. The current healthcare system is paternalistic by nature and focused on allocation of scarce resources to patients. When we present holistic health resources in a structured framework, we can create an ever-expanding ecosystem of relevant resources that can be brought to bear on behalf of consumers when needed and with the most effective communications methods.

Sarah may live in an economically depressed area and may have difficulty completing tasks others take for granted, like getting to work, locating nutritious food, or keeping her children safe. But Sarah, like 81 percent of Americans, owns a smartphone.[25] Through that one device, think of the possibilities of providing Sarah an organized set of holistic health resources, through texts, calls, recorded calls, emails, and apps. Imagine Sarah has one carefully personalized itinerary that offers her a curated assembly of resources specific to her needs: available food programs, grocery delivery services, transportation schedules and options, diabetes support, after-school programs, adult education courses, parenting groups for single mothers. Think of the robust features the right systematic framework could provide her. If Sarah has ready access to such resources and myriad others, couldn't the way she answers the question "What is your health status?" tomorrow be entirely different than how she answers it today?

Technology alone cannot solve the demands of health optimization, as we'll discuss in chapter 9, but the digital age does offer the opportunity to transform the way we think about health when we create the proper framework. No matter the power of technological innovation, what a framework can offer won't have any value if we can't get people to apply it to their lives, and that is where we turn next.

CHAPTER 7

ACTIVATING CONSUMERS TO ACHIEVE HEALTH OPTIMIZATION

This chapter may require the most patience and perseverance to understand. The ideas brought together here have eluded the healthcare industry, not so much from a conceptual standpoint, but because they are difficult to execute. Before developing the underpinnings, I'll give you the summary. Consumer activation in healthcare occurs when three things happen. First, the consumer becomes aware that a resource that is available and relevant to them exists. Second, the consumer gets access and is "connected" to that resource. And third, the consumer completes an action or series of actions to improve their health. Sounds simple in concept, right? But as we think about the myriad types of health improvement resources, how to connect the right ones to the right consumers, and what actions should be taken when and in what order (and using which communications modality), it can become mind-boggling! Let's break it down to see how we can create a personalized health optimization plan, or what I refer to as a personalized health itinerary, for each individual, using durable frameworks and the power of information technology.

Applying Learnings from Internet Success Stories

Because we are entirely accustomed to considering ourselves consumers in the many transactions of our daily lives, we're completely familiar with the terminology "adoption and engagement," even if we never use the words to describe our own behavior. The terms adoption and engagement, as applied in commerce, are most easily seen in use of social media and online shopping. There, adoption means that somebody is signing up for a program, such as becoming an Amazon prime member, a Costco member, or a Netflix subscriber. Adoption also happens when you enroll in one of the reward card programs most of us have filling our wallets or purses. "Adopting" is equally familiar and occurs when opening an Instagram, Facebook, or LinkedIn account and developing a profile. You are now *connected* to a platform and ready for action.

Engagement in online retail and social media refers to the consumer actively making purchases, posting to social media accounts, or interacting with content, comments, reviews, likes and dislikes, or emoticons. Engagement is measured in terms of how much time you spend online, often gauged by your monthly average use (MAU) or daily average use (DAU), and other metrics that track your purchase volume, your number of posts, the time you spend on a site, and the like. Engagement is also measured by the volume of consumer touches or transactions on a given platform by an individual. The major tech players are particularly good at increasing the number of consumer touches by integrating their platforms with other companies in a way that is convenient to you. But this convenience may be accompanied at a price. You may fail to realize that if you've chosen to sign into a mobile application with a Facebook or Google account, for example, you have to some extent agreed to let personal and transactional data about you become a currency for marketing. We see the manifestations of how deeply intertwined these convenient engagements of our cyber lives become when the products we have looked at begin stalking us in our phone apps, alongside our email, and everywhere we go online.

For reasons that have been explained in this book relating to the complexity of healthcare and the previous lack of comprehensive consumer frameworks—and also because of healthcare privacy issues to be addressed in chapter 9—there has been little equivalent of using, let alone measuring, adoption and engagement in healthcare. And yet we know that the healthcare industry in the United States has built a powerful $3.6 trillion transactional machine of healthcare services and goods.[26] Returning to the sentiment I used in chapter 4 when I introduced the concept that healthcare users are *sometimes* patients and *always* consumers, as we think about consumer adoption and engagement, even considering how nonhelpful some nonhealthcare examples are, I'm again of the mind, "If you can't beat them, join them!" Because what I propose is about helping people rather than selling them things, I'm not talking about healthcare improvement resources "stalking" you while you browse the internet. But we do need to consider how the application of interactive information technology can help ensure that resources relevant to improving your health are put in front of you in a timely way.

Turning our unifying equation into consumer activation is a worthwhile endeavor. Let's look again at the denominator, or the inputs to our health.

$$H_V = \frac{\text{Health Status (person or population)}}{\text{Clinical Care ("omics") + Daily Living (SDoH)}}$$

In the last chapter, we developed the taxonomy of a year-in-the-life to think about what can and will happen in the denominator over the course of a year. Understanding the consumer point of view and what problem they are trying to solve is critical to achieving consumer activation. But we also need to step back and think about who is trying to get us to adopt and engage in healthcare, and why they want that to occur. In online retail it's clear why Amazon, Walmart, and Travelocity want us to engage. And in social media and search, even though many consumers of these "free" platforms don't realize that they and their data are the currency, the advertising via technology model is also clear. In healthcare the reasons to drive digital engagement are less mature and a bit fuzzier.

The good news is that healthcare-related entities partner with consumers for clinical care, and they are increasingly seeking to support us in our daily living as well. These include health plans, health services providers, employers, pharmacies, and public and community organizations and institutions. Unlike the clear objectives of the internet giants, each of these healthcare-related entities have differing and sometimes conflicting objectives that confuse consumers. In very general terms, health plans and employers are trying to drive efficient usage of expensive clinical care resources and ensure effective utilization management to control costs. Conversely, health services providers and pharmacies want to drive higher utilization of their services and goods. Meanwhile, public and community organizations try to efficiently distribute and connect clinical care and daily living resources efficiently across specific populations while overcoming negative social determinants that make it difficult to ensure that disadvantaged individuals can be connected to

> Consumers unintentionally get ripped apart by uncoordinated, competing, and nonholistic efforts to get their attention.

health improvement resources and take action. The competing forces to engage consumers in healthcare are powerful and ferocious, and consumers have unwittingly been caught in the whirlwind. In other words, healthcare consumers unintentionally get ripped apart by uncoordinated, competing, and nonholistic efforts to get their attention.

Sounds bad, huh? But if we take a lesson from the internet giants, we can see that having clearly defined objectives for consumer interaction leads to massive adoption and engagement. And so we need to systematically identify the common ground of the different healthcare entities and use these to pivot competing forces onto a common framework. Going back to my introduction, to do so requires that innovation be steeped in tradition, as you are not going to pull out the underpinnings of a $3.6 trillion established industry. Remember, the internet giants learned from traditional physical retail and analog advertising that occurred for many years in order to transform that former world into today's digital retail and advertising world. But even so, remember that the physical and analog world that preceded this did not disappear, and we now enjoy a hybrid digital-physical world.

The Eight Common Stripes of Healthcare Consumer Interaction

I have been fortunate to spend over thirty years in the healthcare industry working in and with nearly every type of healthcare entity. I've been an executive or board member for health plans, hospitals, physician groups, pharmacies, and community organizations. Through collaboration and arm wrestling with my talented colleagues over the years, we have been able to create a systematic set of "reasons" that any healthcare-related entity would want to activate consumers. When doing systems design—and that's what I do—the goal is to ensure that you aren't missing a significant component of a system that impacts the other components. In other words, a good systems design has to be holistic according to the problem it is trying to address. In our case, we want to make sure that we understand and categorize the types of health improvement resources that support health optimization. And, accordingly, we must understand the reasons that any healthcare-related entity might need to make consumers aware of the resources, connect them to the resources, and support consumer actions (and interactions) with those resources.

After years of mind-numbing analyses, industry leader collaborations, trial and error implementations, and arguments with just about everybody I have worked with, the result is what I refer to as the eight common stripes of consumer interaction. I call them "stripes" because they span time. Specifically, they can be considered over the year-in-the-life of a consumer with one lens. They can also be viewed through the lens of any of the healthcare-related entities. Let's see how these different lenses can be peacefully and productively brought together in a common focus.

Here are the categories of the eight common stripes of consumer interaction:

- Support general health and well-being

- Manage chronic conditions

- Navigate people into, out of, and between clinical episodes

- Prevent acute and chronic illness

- Reduce gaps in care where best practices are known

- Provide general communications on healthcare topics such as health literacy or health benefits

- Manage compliance, risk, and preferences including data privacy

- Grow customers and retain/expand the customer relationship

Now try for a moment to see through the lenses of the various healthcare industry players. You may not be a health plan expert, but do you see anything on this list that doesn't make sense for a health plan? How about for health providers such as hospitals and physician groups? What about if you are a retail pharmacy? If you are a state or local government entity or a not-for-profit focused on a high-needs population, do you see anything that doesn't make sense? And finally, if you are thinking as a consumer, it's likely you will find the first six stripes, and perhaps the seventh, to be clearly relevant. While you have to acknowledge that you are a "customer" of the healthcare entities, is there anything on this list you would find objectionable regarding you or your family members taking actions in order to achieve and sustain your highest health status?

Another way to think about the eight stripes is displayed in the picture on the following page. This picture allows us to think about how often over the course of a year we might engage with each of these types of resources.

As you might surmise, the frequency of certain stripe interactions for Fred—a senior with an increasing burden of health conditions—is going to be very different from that of Sam. But I hope you can see that our proposed framework allows healthcare entities to assemble or curate different types of health resources for each stripe and then, based on personalization, ensure that the right resources are getting to the right person at the right time.

Let's get a little deeper understanding of each of the stripes before we discuss how they can create a natural path to increased consumer activation.

The Eight Common Stripes of Consumer Interaction

Growth & Retention

Compliance & Risk Management

Prevention | Gaps in Care | Prevention | Gaps in Care

Pre Episode | Post Episode | Pre Episode | Post Episode

Chronic Condition Management

General Health & Well-Being

Sponsor Communications

Jan → Dec

Preepisodic, Interepisodic, and Postepisodic Activities

These are classic interactions related to our clinical care visits. We are used to these kinds of interactions because they are "patient" transactions. Clinical care providers need an ability to reach out to a consumer ahead of an appointment or procedure so the consumer can take necessary actions to make and keep the appointment and know what to expect. Obviously, you interact with the caregiver during the appointment, procedure, or test, and then as soon as you conclude that visit, you're either postepisodic or interepisodic, meaning that you have additional visits related to that healthcare episode. You have follow-up tasks to complete—taking medication, treating a surgical incision, altering your diet during recovery or after diagnosis, attending therapy, making a follow-up appointment, and so on. You might only be in your doctor's presence for five minutes, but the full set of tasks related to that episode will need to be integrated into the other 99 percent of your life. Not only might there be actions you must take for the best outcome of the episode, but during this time the provider may also wish to maintain some level of ongoing longitudinal contact or relationship with you, if only to let you know they are "thinking" about you. Your employer or health plan also has an interest in how you navigate in and out of these clinical care episodes, as well as the outcome and the cost.

Reduction in Gaps of Care

Annual checkups, mammograms, prostate exams, dental cleanings … these clinical encounters are all designed with time intervals to ensure that regular diagnostics and metrics about our health are tracked. Having baseline information can have a huge impact on achieving our optimal health. But unless providers have a systematic methodology of communicating with consumers and knowing whether they have or haven't done these things, gaps in care can easily emerge. Interaction might be as unsophisticated as your dentist sending you a postcard reminder every six months, or your reminders might be digital. But if providers cannot effectively reach out or you fail to schedule your regular appointment, very real medical risks can develop during that care gap. In general, clinical check-ins on things that nearly all health-care professionals, academic institutions, and regulatory agencies agree on are known as evidence-based medicine. In other words, scientific and statistical evidence show that people can maintain better health status if they do certain things at recommended intervals.

Prevention

Our current sickcare system is actually quite good at prevention if and only if healthcare entities can succeed in activating the consumer to participate. Among the most obvious examples of prevention would be immunizations, whether DPT and polio vaccines for children, shingles vaccination for the elderly, or the ubiquitous annual flu shot. Prevention is often a matter of public health. As we have seen with COVID-19 and prior outbreaks, if there's a viral pandemic, creating an awareness campaign that helps consumers understand how to prevent or lower their risk factors can be critical. We've proven that we might be familiar with the importance of frequent and effective handwashing, but we are not at all accustomed to the demands of wearing masks or social distancing. We take a lot of public policy prevention for granted, like chlorine in our water supply or having municipal sewage systems. We tend only to focus on such systems when they fail. If they do fail (ask the residents of Flint, Michigan), we need mechanisms for informing the public and providing them resources for options. Many prevention measures are also evidence based.

Chronic Condition Management

Chronic condition management is exactly what it sounds like. Conditions requiring ongoing management include hypertension, congestive heart failure, and even many types of cancer. Perhaps the classic example in the United States is type 2 diabetes. If you're diagnosed with high hemoglobin A1C, then engaging in a program that, at a minimum, helps you understand what you can do to help yourself from a diet, fitness, alcohol consumption, and sleep standpoint is critical. You need regular access to information and reminders about how to best affect the course of your disease. The more automated reminders or alerts there are, the better, right down to monitoring your blood sugar level so you know when you need an insulin injection or emergency outreach to a medical professional. All chronic conditions have a specific diagnosis and associated risk factors. Many of these risk factors are controllable, but only if the consumer is receiving outreach and is actively engaged. If the information is not provided in the context of their benefit plan or factoring in their local community resources, it is going to be less effective. We once again must consider the individual's social determinants as well as his or her benefit plan. Management of Sarah's diabetes and Fred's wife's breast cancer doesn't happen in the same way, and the outreach to them must know each of them as a person. For example, because Fred's wife has dementia, she will need to be activated through a caregiver. Managing a chronic condition is definitely not an interaction where one size fits all.

General Health and Well-Being

This stripe encompasses all of those things that would not typically be specifically contained in the above four and pertain generally to physical health-related things like your personal level of fitness and mobility, your nutrition, and the monitoring of your standard biometrics. It also includes, very importantly, the broader view of total well-being that involves your management of stress and sleep, your personal relationships, your financial wellness, your mental health, and the types of not-so-nutritional substances you might partake in, like alcohol. Because this is a much broader category of interaction and resource need, and because it is significantly impacted by social determinants, there are comparatively few controls or regulations governing the programs that are available. As a result, there is more opportunity for consumers to be exposed to information and products that might not be in their best interest. Anyone who has tried to research news articles, blogs, and magazine pieces about losing weight (i.e., nutrition) can attest not just to the volume of information available but also to how often what is found is contradictory. The challenge is to sort through the noise and get the right set of resources to the right person, delivered in the right way. But if you understand people's benefits and their social determinants, then you can use good data and information science to direct them to useful resources. Because 70 percent of what drives our health is nonclinical and nongenetic, this category is key, but it has to be multifaceted and it has to work with the other 30 percent—our clinical care. We'll elaborate on this general health and well-being category later in chapter 9.

Customer Growth and Retention

Growth and retention can come in many forms. If you're a hospital provider, you would want to make consumers aware of offerings available in your community. The hospital might want to make local consumers aware of their latest high-tech surgical capabilities, new facilities, or newly hired doctors. A health plan provider will want to remind consumers how insurance can provide peace of mind and partner with you when you become ill. An employer may want to remind employees of the full range of benefits that are part of their compensation package and let them know that they provide resources intended to keep them happy and healthy well beyond what they view as their traditional access to clinical care. Employers recognize that if they can't maintain and communicate a competitive benefits package for employees, they suffer higher attrition rates. Pharmacies want to make sure you fill and refill your prescriptions and ensure you know that they offer other goods and services as well. The goal of all such consumer outreach is to make consumers aware of the value of the entity's offerings and to keep their brand in front of them. And, importantly, because a consumer already has a relationship with a doctor, employer, health plan, pharmacy, and other healthcare entities, this type of advertising doesn't feel like advertising. In healthcare it's often more about reinforcement of trusted brands.

Compliance, Risk, and Preference Management

This is probably the stripe that the fewest people think about, yet it is very important. It also will prove central to the next chapter, where we'll discuss the thorny issues of healthcare data privacy. Compliance and risk management are somewhat known to all consumers, if only through the required communication of HIPAA privacy notifications. There's much, much more to compliance and risk management than HIPAA. Depending on whether you're an actual patient or a prospective patient and depending whether you are on a Medicare plan or an employer self-funded plan, different kinds of permissions and consumer preferences need to be understood, recorded, documented, and applied. As a required starting point, no matter the purpose or form of outreach, all the various health entities need to verify that the person they are trying to contact is the actual person they have reached. They also need to know that this consumer has provided permission to be contacted or to have their data used. Entities need to be sure that no laws are being violated when they reach out. These are essentials of compliance.

Risk management, beyond compliance, shows up in the form of health history questionnaires and risk assessments—used for both underwriting and clinical care planning—and other types of interactive outreach where those doing the outreach are trying to glean some information about an individual. It also includes patient intake or communication initiated by the consumer to provide the healthcare entity information. This could be telling your doctor that you have had a health event unrelated to any chronic condition, diagnostic test, or treatment focus. This is the classic "I know I'm being treated after knee surgery, but now my back hurts" or "Yeah, I've been laid up long enough that I'm probably drinking more alcohol than I usually do to deal with the boredom."

When risk management is initiated by those in the various facets of the healthcare system, they have to be skilled in how such communication reaches the consumer, and they have to be purposeful in how the data that comes from risk assessment is used. But by the same token, the compliance and risk management stripe provides a rich underpinning of how information can be appropriately used to support the other seven stripes. Done well, a platform that includes mechanisms for engaging the consumer in assessing health risks can generate data that drive the personalization of the health itinerary for total health and wellness.

General Communication

I know it feels that certainly we've already covered every conceivable kind of outreach. But there remain communications that simply deliver general information. Central among such messages are notifications. Think about it from the perspectives of our various entities, and you see there is a great deal of consumer outreach that doesn't fit into our other stripes. Your employer needs to do simple things like remind you about the upcoming employee picnic, and they have a responsibility to inform you about health-related events like announcements about open enrollment periods for health benefits. Similarly, providers might need to announce community health events or new services or new facilities.

Here is a central additional point: A well-designed system of communicating resources and information must be linked to all the other reasons for outreach we have already discussed. Consumers need coordinated messages. That means communication—whether about a new wing opening at the local clinic, a follow-up to a surgical procedure you recently had, or a push notification that says your blood sugar is elevated and you need insulin—needs to come through an effective channel. Anything less than a coordinated, holistic platform isn't just ineffective and inefficient, but it will also cut consumer participation and undermine their health and total well-being as a result.

> *A well-designed system of communicating resources and information must be linked to all the other reasons for outreach we have already discussed. Consumers need coordinated messages.*

Requirements of an Effective Technology Platform

As you can see, healthcare consumers have a tremendous need for information and resources. And healthcare entities have a wide range of reasons and objectives in connecting information and resources to consumers. While we now have an orderly set of frameworks to think about in relation to a year-in-the-life and the eight common stripes of consumer interaction, we have more to think about in terms of creating an effective healthcare consumer platform that rivals the engagement characteristics of the internet giants and drives consumer activation across both clinical care and daily living. An effective health-care consumer platform needs to create *relevance*, ease of *accessibility* and *value*, and be *easy!* And while I fully understand that in the contemporary landscape of the retail internet, these are all "duh" items, it's truly far more complicated in healthcare if you are going to take a whole person view versus just pushing some fragment of total health and well-being.

Creating technologically based distribution methods can lead to far greater consumer adoption and engagement, so long as what is provided to individual consumers is seen as relevant to their lives. If Sam, a single male Millennial, gets information through his mobile app about mammogram scheduling or pediatric education programs, he's not going to sign up, no matter how beautiful the graphics or how smooth the interface. Similarly, Fred may not be a great candidate for a hard-core, high-impact online fitness program. In order for people to adopt an interactive platform and want to engage with it, there has to be personal relevance. And in healthcare, relevance goes back to the year-in-the-life and an understanding of an individual's benefit plan, his or her current health status, and the problem or concern that needs to be solved. This relevancy is difficult to get correct without daily living and social determinant data.

Ease of accessibility can be thought of in several ways. But as it relates to healthcare, any consumer is going to think about financial accessibility and ask the question of whether a resource being offered is part of their benefit plan or comes at an additional cost. From a platform standpoint, they are also going to think about "how many clicks" does it take for them to get connected to the resource, even if it is relevant. Do they have to enter new information or are they already "known"? As previously stated, the internet giants excel at using an existing profile to make connection to a new thing easy. And of course a consumer wants to understand if the resource is geographically accessible. But geography is better expressed as localization. If a resource has to be accessed in person, that is one issue. For example, if the top pediatric asthma specialty clinic in Sarah's city is more than an hour and four bus transfers away or does not accept Medicaid patients, it loses both relevance and accessibility to her. But even with virtual or online health improvement resources, if the source seems "too far away," "not culturally compatible with me," or "not the local brand I trust," then accessibility is also hindered. There is a reason people develop trust with their local hardware store. Nonetheless, for some types of resources and some types of people, access can mean connecting an individual to enroll in a virtual diabetes program like Livongo or a nutrition management program like Weight Watchers as easily as putting something in your shopping cart on Amazon or Walmart online.

Next, the resources that come through the platform must provide value. There are lots of ways individuals measure value. For some, and this can be useful when we think about consumer activation of healthcare, value literally means providing something for free. For others, getting something for free actually removes the value, and they go looking for the "catch." What I think is a good value is different than what you think is a good value. But again, given the myriad types of resources that can be connected to consumers through a personalized platform, we can't get too narrow. The concept of "free" takes on a different context if the reason it is free is that access to the resource is part of a benefit plan and the relevancy and accessibility of the resource are intelligently communicated as tailored for you. The concept of "incentives and rewards"—a vital part of a healthcare consumer platform—can take on the context of "if you complete actions that improve your health, you get rewarded" in contrast to retail thinking, where the more you buy, the more points or rewards you get. In healthcare, like in retail, relating rewards to activity is a form of gaming to drive behavior, but the purposes are very different. And the value of engaging with health improvement can be underscored when the rewards tie back to the actions themselves, such as having a fitness program membership fee waived or getting a premium reduction for completing a specific set of year-in-the-life tasks early in the year.

Even if health improvement resources are teed up in a way that is relevant, accessible, and valuable, it still has to be easy! The connection to consumers has to integrate as seamlessly as possible into daily living. Online retailers understand the power of ease of adoption and engagement. This is why the outdoor enthusiast receives a daily email from REI with a link that takes them immediately to a sport for which they have made past purchases, or a HelloFresh meal user receives a text message with a 10 percent off coupon on meals. When the outreach arrives on a Saturday morning as you're thinking about heading to the grocery store but don't yet have a meal plan for the week, it's easy to click the link. You don't even have to get out your wallet.

A quote attributed to Aesop, the famous Greek fabulist, is as follows: "After all is said and done, more is said than done." In healthcare getting a consumer to take actions and proactively participate in improving his or her own health is challenging, no matter consumers' best intentions. And getting a consumer to take action with timeliness and consistency is more challenging still. How often have you had a health professional suggest the importance of an action that could have clear positive impact—floss daily, cut a problem food out of your diet, exercise 150 minutes a week, take time to do breathing exercises or meditate? Yet, despite our best intentions, how many follow through with such advice? We might do well for a week or two, but how successful are we at making change, no matter how simple, part of an altered lifestyle? Our lives are busy, and habits are entrenched. That's why they are called habits. There are occasional "insta-changes," epiphany-driven exceptions, of course. But even when serious consequences are at stake, most of us have better intentions than implementation. Let's say our doctor or nutritionist talked with us about the benefits of comparing sugar to fiber in the food we consume, gave us some nutritional literature, and suggested that we go home and read the labels in our refrigerator. We probably see the wisdom in this advice and tell ourselves we'll get right on it. But when we get home, one of the kids is late for practice, and the other one is throwing a fit. There's a leak under the kitchen sink. The neighbor trimmed a hedge on our side of the property line. It's a week before Christmas, and we haven't started shopping. And not to make light but to underscore the power of distraction, there's a worldwide pandemic. That's daily living.

I believe there is an answer to the conundrum of proactively taking actions to improve our health through the very type of platform we have described. In healthcare it seems that

> If a platform can tee up relevant, accessible, and valuable health improvement programming that is personalized to an individual consumer and is easy and rewarding … it is going to get traction!

everybody wants to talk about behavior change. We could have a protracted discussion about the realistic prospects of true intrinsic behavior change and what it means. But that's not a debate we have time for in this book, and we might not reach firm conclusions if we did. For our purposes, my point is that if a platform can tee up relevant, accessible, and valuable health improvement programming that is personalized to an individual consumer and is easy and rewarding … it is going to get traction! That thought takes us to the personal health itinerary.

The Personal Health Itinerary

When I was a kid, my family often drove between my hometown of Boulder, Colorado, and Chicago, Illinois, to visit my grandparents from both sides of the family. This is a less than riveting journey of approximately one thousand miles. But to my delight, my parents reached out to AAA and got what was a called a TripTik. It was this spiral-bound book in which each page represented a short segment of the long journey, and it included callouts for items of interest, gas stations, restaurants, and hotels along the way. In short, it took a long journey with a significant number of potential variables along the way and made it tolerable and actionable. And, fascinatingly, even though we repeated the same trip each year, instead of each occurrence becoming more boring than the last, the TripTik exposed us to different resources that allowed for the experience to become more meaningful each time. The TripTik might well be responsible for my penchant for breaking down problems and doing systems analysis.

Fast-forward to the digital age, and we still have the challenge of a healthcare journey that I have described in a year-in-the-life, with some components that get repeated every year and some that change as the years go by. While it's quite a bit harder to navigate the journey to achieve optimal health and well-being than it is to drive on interstate highways—and the variables of different types of healthcare entities, the year-in-the-life taxonomy, and the eight common consumer interaction categories create billions of combinations and permutations versus the hundreds of possibilities of where to stop on my cross-country trips—it's still about breaking down a journey into manageable and executable pieces. The truth is that we live in a world where people want simplicity to get from point A to point B. Google this, buy that, just give me the result now! But have you noticed the people and organizations that undertake the complex efforts to create simplicity are the recipients of a disproportionate amount of value?

In healthcare, if point A is you and your current health status as it exists today, and point B is anytime in the future, the pathways to that future are not a single straight line. But if we apply the principles in this book, it is also not an infinite number of lines.

Providing consumers with a personalized health itinerary that is relevant, accessible, valuable, and easy is a high calling!

> *Providing consumers with a personalized health itinerary that is relevant, accessible, valuable, and easy is a high calling!*

Over my thirty years in healthcare, I have watched 100 percent of every well-meaning healthcare organization, including technology companies trying to solve healthcare problems, essentially get bogged down and worn out trying to piece together all the moving parts. To be clear, this includes highly successful companies that have great leaders, are truly innovative, and have brilliant people and massive amounts of capital.

Creating a personal health itinerary for an individual that will guide them toward their highest health status means that we must identify a clear and comprehensive set of health improvement resources for that person. Before resources can be personalized to a consumer, they must first be curated. Curation of health improvement resources is similar to our local hardware store owner with many years of experience deciding what type of inventory to put on his shelves and organizing it in a way that makes it easy to find. Of course, if you want to provide comprehensive solutions, you need to make sure that you have a sufficient number of offerings in each different "aisle" (e.g., the eight stripe categories) to properly serve the entirety of your population. When you then connect the right subset of your curated resources to the individual consumer so that they can complete actions to improve their health, that's the health itinerary. Simple enough, right?

In order to connect resources, the consumer has to know what resources exist. Even if the store aisles might be fully stocked with things that could be useful and relevant to you, if you don't know they exist, their presence is meaningless. Navigating a Walmart Supercenter with no logic in the store layout, no signage, and no employees to consult would probably send customers back to the parking lot as fast as the electronic doors can reopen. Once you are aware such curated resources exist, you need a workflow capability to be able to complete actions over a modality that works for you. We each have our preferred method of interaction and receiving information. Apps, texts, chatbots, interactive digital voice calls ... we must make all the communication tools at our disposal available so consumers can pick the ones that work for their individual needs and tastes. Then, whatever modality they choose, it has to move them along through whatever process is required. Unlike making a purchase at Amazon or Walmart, where you click once and the delivery of a physical good is initiated, in healthcare the consumer must take a series of steps. Because transactions are not singular, the steps we need to take must be ordered and, if appropriate, scheduled for action and completion. What also adds complexity is that health and well-being are dynamic. As we offer consumers a purposefully thorough, holistic, curated set of resources to support them in their daily living, we need to make sure that these resources reflect their ever-changing health status. We also need to make sure that the resources we curate are kept up to date as both clinical and daily living innovations occur.

As you might expect, there is much more I could explain regarding how to break down and curate the specific resources needed to accomplish the eight stripes of consumer interaction over the year-in-the-life of a consumer. And there are specific solutions that deliver the highest value for health plans, providers, pharmacies, employers, and public and community entities. Simplifying this complexity into consumer activation solutions for healthcare entities is the work of my colleagues at Welltok. Just like Google made search easy and Amazon made online shopping orderly and easy, Welltok is making consumer activation orderly and easier. What's important is that you understand that achieving a personalized health itinerary for clinical care and daily living, personalized by "omics" and social determinants, is possible. And that much of the complexity in producing the simplicity is now invented, even if at an early stage, as compared to potential.

You would think that the breakthrough of consumer activation through personalized health itineraries would instantly capture the attention of the healthcare industry because there is now a platform for the 99 percent of our lives to complement the 1 percent. But as we will see in the next section of the book, there are still a number of distractions that need to be overcome or better leveraged to create the transformation from reactive sickcare to proactive total health and well-being.

Part IV: For Better, for Worse

Producing the Best Health Outcomes by
Putting Data to Work for Good Purposes

CHAPTER 8

DATA PRIVACY CONCERNS IN CONTEXT

Sometimes it feels like we can't wake up without reading about a company suffering a security breach or encountering a headline about how a social media company is embattled in a privacy dispute. The headlines do make people worry, which is understandable, even if appearances are likely inflated beyond real concerns. There is no doubt that we live in an age of increasing cybercomplexity. The amount of data about us as individuals and the volume of interactions stored on corporate computer networks or exchanged on the internet has dramatically changed over the past two decades. The rate with which these data transactions occur, whether people are searching for information, purchasing things online, or sharing communications with one another and through social media, is increasing at an exponential rate. Clearly our capacity to keep up with the implications of such transactions is getting harder, not easier. At the risk of sounding crass, my response is "Deal with it in an informed and realistic way. This isn't a trend we're going to change."

Total Well-Being Requires Clinical and Consumer Data

I firmly believe that the fusion of consumer and clinical data is the best opportunity we have available as a society to drive the greatest health status improvement of our overall population at the highest level of economic return on investment. Why? Because the data required already exists. Equally obvious, the kinds of mechanisms I've proposed for helping individual consumers achieve optimal health are highly dependent on rich data sets about people. If we are truly to personalize consumers' healthcare needs, we've got to know more about them than their diagnoses ... at least as much as we know about Sarah, Fred, María, and Sam. So how do we balance the need for useful consumer data with a need to ensure privacy?

I firmly believe that the fusion of consumer and clinical data is the best opportunity we have available as a society to drive the greatest health status improvement of our overall population at the highest level of economic return on investment.

Let's face it, many people do worry about the sanctity of what they regard as private parts of their lives. Healthcare is a trust environment. We all understand that when we sit down and discuss our health concerns with our personal physician, we are placing our total trust in that professional to respect the confidentiality of what we share and to restrict use of such information to actions that will heal us and help us. Yet, depending on our generational or cultural backgrounds, sometimes sharing our health lives even with a licensed, trusted provider remains intimidating. Many people can't begin to imagine an environment in which we expand the circle of trust regarding who we ask to be responsible for and protective of what we share about ourselves. It is an understandable fear. Yet it is one we've got to combat if we are truly going to reap the benefits in trying to help people experience their highest health status and total well-being.

There are two perplexing challenges that have to be addressed in terms of understanding healthcare data privacy: first, the unlocking and sharing of clinical data, and second, the application and integration of consumer data that is not specifically clinically related. As we've discussed in earlier chapters, the latter data represents daily living and social determinants and paints a picture of 99 percent or more of our lives. Let's take these on one at a time.

Regarding data in clinical settings, we only have to go back two decades to find the normative state of data storage was paper files with doctors' notes or printouts of lab and test results stored in manila files, all hand managed. Moreover, your individual health record was contained within a single provider, and if you wanted to share that data with another provider or change providers, you literally had to get a hard copy of these files and physically transport them. As a result, the security and privacy of such data was a physical situation based upon who could walk into the file rooms of a physician's office or a hospital record room. Sure, the wrong bad actor could gain access to the file room and retrieve very personal information, but consider the likelihood of suffering a loss of your privacy in such an environment compared to the scaled reality of the internet age. The likelihood of the wrong people accessing your information felt remote in this bygone era.

While largely secure, such archaic records systems were incredibly inefficient, and they often had negative repercussions on clinical care treatment. Too often such inefficiency contributed to patients receiving the wrong medications, suffering allergic reactions, or being assailed by complications arising from misdiagnoses or problematic drug interactions. These problems far outweighed any privacy concerns. It wasn't until the passage of the American Recovery and Reinvestment Act of 2009 that the healthcare industry was formally legislated and incented to adopt the use of electronic health records. The idea was that records could be shared across different providers with what we now call interoperability. Interoperability is desirable but comes with perplexing challenges because of the large number of different electronic health record software companies that are all trying to differentiate the value of their products and, often, protect the value of the data that flows through their software systems. Accordingly, the current status of easily sharing data about a person's diagnoses, procedures, medication history, lab results, and biometrics to inform the provider about the patient's past is still a work in progress.

Electronic medical records data remains an imperfect science, but in terms of data privacy, one that has reached a relatively mature state. Slowly we have gathered patient data into two general groupings: clinical data and claims data. Clinical data sets include details of medical procedures, lab work, imaging, clinical notes, and those things that require specialized clinical education to understand and apply inside of clinical organizations. By contrast, when providers transmit data to insurance entities in order to get paid, we call that claims data. Some refer to the two data types as clinical data and administrative data. Both data types are protected under a set of laws known as HIPAA. The average consumer is most familiar with HIPAA through the acknowledgment forms they sign at providers and through the privacy notices they routinely receive. In most cases, when you enroll in health insurance, you are also authorizing the use of your data under HIPAA guidelines. The existence of a signed HIPAA authorization in no way ensures that your desire to allow the transfer of clinical information among providers will actually occur, but it does make it possible because you have established a permission chain. HIPAA is imperfect and insufficient, but there are appropriate pressures and many initiatives in the industry to continue to maintain privacy and access rules for clinical data. Because the underlying digital technology platforms for clinical data transactions are well established, the interoperability of that data should continue to improve over time and be accessible more conveniently to your providers and you.

But if it took us well into the twenty-first century to reach a point where we have started to make interoperability real from a technology standpoint, imagine the challenge of replicating such a system to use consumer data in healthcare. Remember, we're only in the presence of clinical providers for less than 1 percent of our lives. The other 99 percent of our lives, daily living, accounts for a whole lot of data. And that's a whole lot of data to think about in terms of data privacy! Yet we must solve the problem of bringing daily living data together with clinical data in order to create an environment where optimized health can occur.

> *The other 99 percent of our lives, daily living, accounts for a whole lot of data. And that's a whole lot of data to think about in terms of data privacy!*

The Digital World Already Knows You

Fortunately, even if sometimes to our chagrin, the world has become highly adept at capturing data about people that's not healthcare related. In other words, the data already exists, so it's out there, and any privacy concerns regarding it logically do not originate with new applications. Information collected about us includes government data like federal, state, and local data generated from the census, the IRS, property recording and property taxing authorities, automobile registrations, environmental surveys, localized demographics, and local community social services organizations. Additionally, we've already drawn numerous examples from the retail sector's voluminous data collection capabilities. Through shopping transaction data and catalog browsing data, and by employing data generated through loyalty programs, retailers are astute at capturing and applying data specifically to an identifiable individual. Companies that provide search capabilities, such as Google, Microsoft, and Apple, are able to capture information about an individual's interests, and they are able to tie that information to the individual by offering such things as free email and other services that allow them to connect online activity to a specific person. Social media further provides not only information about specific individuals but builds a social graph of relationships so that they have knowledge not just of the individual and their interests and conversations but also of whom that individual associates with. This allows social network providers the ability to know your network of relationships and the key influencers within those relationships. Your smartphone alone contains a treasure trove of information about you. My point is this: While I don't wish in any way to downplay the responsibility a more holistic health platform would have to protecting your privacy, let's face it—do you realistically have more reason to fear a hacker breaking into a professionally managed secure server designed to support actions that could help you be healthier or losing your phone in the back seat of an Uber?

As I've said earlier, none of these points of data collection or the entities that do the gathering are in and of themselves nefarious. The Uber driver who finds your phone probably isn't either. The reason we get most of the headlines is because data that was intended for productive purposes falls into the hands of bad actors who use it to exploit individuals, organizations, or even countries. But that is a data security issue more so than a data privacy issue. We will not cover data security here, but I will give some thoughts on how consumer and clinical data in healthcare can be more protected even if hacked or stolen. Further, it's not the purpose of this book to define what is or isn't appropriate use of personal data because ultimately, just like people in the 1980s had to decide whether to list their phone numbers and addresses in the phone book, people today have to make conscious decisions about how and for what purpose they want to expose their identities. Making personal choices about data privacy is another aspect of being an active consumer—in healthcare or otherwise. Let's make sure that consumers can make those choices and establish a verifiable and updatable permission chain so that those choices can be applied and updated. This ties back to the compliance, risk management, and preference stripe from the previous chapter.

My personal view is that rather than focusing on privacy concerns around healthcare data as a starting point, we should be concentrating on what nonclinical data about people can be the most helpful, when it is combined with clinical data, so that they can achieve and sustain their highest health at the lowest cost. There is an abundance of such data available. If we could access and properly apply social determinant data—things like a person's financial wherewithal, their living circumstances, their access to transportation, and other similar facts of their lives—we could empower organizations that are partnering with them as both patients and consumers. One challenge is that organizations already in possession of the greatest amount of such data use business models that generate revenue through advertising. The goal of such business models is to use data aimed at persuading consumers to purchase more goods or services. What gets discussed in those boardrooms is revenue and profit margins in their existing business models, with a constant strategic drumbeat that says, "Healthcare is a really big industry and health is the most important thing ... we should do something meaningful in healthcare!" But those companies almost always think first about how their technologies can apply to clinical data. That's okay; it's just not broad enough thinking. The true underlying problem isn't so much about data privacy as it is advancing the underlying purpose of data applicability.

Frankly, I wish we were at a point where any of the healthcare entities on which we are dependent had such great data about a person that we actually had to worry about its misuse. Instead, today's reality is that healthcare providers have virtually no data beyond the strictly clinical. Health plans have virtually no data other than claims data, basic demographics, and some health risk assessment information that's been self-reported by their members. And employers have to walk a fine line because while they have extremely good access to communication with their employees, they can't put themselves in a position where they're seeing detailed medical information. We're ages behind where we should be given the technological capabilities and data sources available.

What we require is a new type of thinking that enables consumer data to be collected and classified in an orderly way and applied to situations that are in the best interests of that consumer's total health. The application of properly applied consumer data intelligence is precisely what underlies a healthcare consumer activation platform. The goal is to help plan out the year-in-the-life of a consumer within the reality of their benefit plan in partnership with their health plan and employer (if they have employer-based insurance) and then apply available data about an individual's social determinants to help connect them to the best personalized and localized health improvement resources for them. We need a healthcare world where a physician interacting with a patient has enough social determinant information to know whether a drug they wish to prescribe or physical therapy they recommend is accessible to the patient financially and geographically. Might Sarah be willing to share information about herself if it means her daughter's pediatrician can recommend a free clinic focused on adolescent asthma self-management that is within walking distance or one bus ride from their apartment? Wouldn't María find value in her employer providing her supportive resources with the recognition that she needs to attend appointments with her aging parents?

Privacy is something we should value, and we should not take its protection lightly. But if we can develop a system that focuses on the best interests of consumers, we have so much to gain in realizing a healthier population that we shouldn't let worries over privacy curtail us from pushing the development of a more holistic itinerary. It's certainly not impossible to protect data while

The key is to keep the goal—the best possible health at the best possible price, personalized to individuals—firmly in mind.

still putting it to work in smarter ways. Using it wisely can help all of us. The key is to keep the goal—the best possible health at the best possible price, personalized to individuals—firmly in mind.

Exceptions Should Not Set the Rules

Despite occasional faults in the use of healthcare data, the current system is geared toward producing the best outcomes for those in its care and figuring out better ways to apply data and technology.

Many entities in the US healthcare system refer to the pursuit of the "triple aim": improving the experience of care, improving the health of populations, and reducing per capita costs of healthcare.[27] And some organizations add a fourth goal to create a "quadruple aim," and that fourth goal can vary but often alludes to establishing better equity of resource distribution across populations or serving some other higher purpose. These goals all require more—and more integrated—data, not less. And consumers need a mixture of clinical and applied consumer data to make choices about the economics of their benefit plans and how it relates to their access to clinical and other health improvement resources. At present, most consumers have some choice in the health plan they choose. The options may feel somewhat limited, but there is typically at least a range of choices among plans that employers provide, and those in the private insurance market have a choice in offerings, although these are—as we have discussed—limited by financial constraints. For those in government-sponsored plans, there are generally choices between traditional government offerings in Medicare or Medicaid and managed care offerings through private insurers. I think we can all be comforted by the fact that despite whatever frustrations exist within such plans, they have been developed with the best interests of their participants in mind, and with regulatory oversight. Remember, these benefit plans in a year-in-the-life of a consumer start to define the boundaries of data flow and the resources that can be attached to an individual. The framework of a benefit plan positions the consumer to make a significant series of choices. Every time a consumer chooses one physician over another or one pharmacy over the next, they are exerting a choice, including where their data flows.

Of course, there will always be some bad actors—providers who might use their position of licensing and information power to perform blatantly unnecessary or fraudulent medical procedures, or pharmacies that perpetuate unnecessary refills to drive revenue. But we shouldn't drive data sharing or data privacy policy based on the exceptional cases. We have to let our regulatory framework root out those bad actors, and frankly they can use more consumer data to identify these patterns. The firewalls that already exist on the clinical side should continue to exist as we expand beyond clinical data.

To be clear, controlling who sees your data is different than controlling who should be allowed to apply your data for your potential benefit. While it's certainly the case that no diagnosis made by your doctor today should ever reach your employer unless you choose to tell them, if you were ill and a potential subject for a clinical trial, even if you hadn't specifically authorized the use of your data for that purpose, wouldn't you like to know that? And while you might not even want your friends and family to know about your debt or personal relationship issues, wouldn't you want outreach on resources that could help you if your data suggested that these were problem areas for you? A categorized flow of available data will allow healthcare entities to piece together a more holistic vision of their patients, members, and employees. More data, organized and classified, can produce a whole person picture that enables every one of those entities to provide the best possible recommendations or services to help you achieve and sustain your highest status of health and well-being. Whether you choose to engage with these resources or not still remains your choice, but how can you choose something you don't know about?

As it relates to innovative use of technology, keep in mind that the flow of data that can support an individual consumer doesn't always mean that the identity of a person has to be known in order to make it useful. From a security standpoint, nearly all sensitive data in healthcare is required to be encrypted, which basically means you cannot read it unless you have the encryption key to unlock it. When data is completely disconnected from the individual it applies to, that is called anonymization. It's good for studying aggregated patterns but not helpful to the problems we are solving in this book. There are at least two other techniques, one called pseudonymization and one known as tokenization, that allows us to have rich amounts of data about an individual without directly attaching that data to the identity of a person. Using these techniques, should a database be hacked or fall into the wrong hands, the data could not be tied to individual people without another source of information that ties the pseudonyms or tokens to identifiable data. Tokenization allows authorized people and entities to "reassemble" data, with permission, in the best interests of a consumer. I was involved in the earliest application of these data privacy techniques, and they work very well if properly implemented. However, it also suggests that there needs to be a trusted entity (or entities) that can pull your otherwise anonymous data together.

A next step in accomplishing such a climate is to follow the lead of the European Union and its development of the General Data Protection Regulation (GDPR). The core construct of GDPR is that the consumer grants permissions through a data trust broker and that data trust broker keeps track of who does or does not have the right to use and apply this data and for what purposes. It operates out of a belief that individuals' data is owned by them, not by the entities in possession of that data. This permission set is dynamic and can be reviewed by the consumer on a regular basis so that they can see how the use of their data is benefiting them or make changes to the permissions they grant. GDPR requires that all personally identifiable information be anonymized unless otherwise permitted. In the United States, California and Massachusetts have crafted consumer data protection legislation largely modeled on GDPR. Under such systems some people may still make suboptimal decisions regarding their own privacy, but at least they are provided the opportunity to make such choices. One final point is that in those states that have crafted updated data protection legislation, data that can be shared under HIPAA regulations does not require explicit permission by the consumer, so as not to impede clinical data sharing.

I'm not naïve about the need to establish both technological and regulatory controls on access to personal data. But the legislators and lawyers need help in understanding what we are trying to accomplish. In the end it comes down what we discussed at the outset of this chapter and throughout this book. As we develop a better model, we need those who deeply understand how the US healthcare system functions to think about how expanded consumer data can best be integrated with clinical data and then how it can best be protected. There are ways of accomplishing this today that violate no laws or regulations, and I have spent a great deal of time and effort stepping through the minefields of well-intended restrictions that ultimately end up restricting progress across the broader healthcare landscape. We must create a climate where data privacy that honors a consumer's intent in a trustful environment is standard in all aspects of the digital world we live in. But no part of that world is more important than enabling data to flow and come together in a manner that can help every person achieve and sustain their highest expression of health and well-being.

CHAPTER 9

SILICON VALLEY CAN HELP BUT WILL NOT SOLVE HEALTHCARE

One of the greatest differentiators that sets the United States apart from many, if not most, other countries is our capacity to deploy capital in pursuit of innovation and profit. In the current age, capitalism might best be embodied in the concept we label as Silicon Valley, and here of course I am using Silicon Valley as a metonym for the larger high-tech sector of the economy. The data that was the focus of the last chapter largely is stored within the systems built by the companies we associate with Silicon Valley. Nearly every American has no trouble naming the big five tech companies, for they dominate much of our lives: Amazon, Apple, Facebook, Google, and Microsoft. But many others are nearly omnipresent: Twitter, Airbnb, Salesforce, Uber, and all those that actually power them—like Intel, Oracle, Samsung, Broadcom, and Qualcomm. We're all hopelessly dependent upon a world filled with tech companies with names that sound like characters from 1970s science fiction TV shows.

For the needs of this book, standing alongside the technological, data-driven "new" economy we think of when we use the term Silicon Valley are the familiar incumbent organizations we have in mind when we think about the traditional healthcare industry. These include the for-profit and nonprofit insurance entities, the employer groups who provide health benefits for their employees, hospitals and healthcare systems, retail pharmacies and medical supply firms, and big pharma and biotech companies where much of research and development occurs. Whether or not you buy their products or use their services, you've probably heard of most of the following example names: United Health Group, Blue Cross Blue Shield, Ascension Health, Cigna, Humana, Kaiser, CVS-Aetna, Anthem, Eli Lilly, Pfizer, HCA, Walgreens, and Rite-Aid.

In contrast to the previous entities, most of the vital companies that supply information technology that actually powers the $3.5 trillion healthcare system are not household names. Healthcare information technology (HCIT) companies like EPIC, Cerner, Athena, Allscripts, NextGen, Cognizant, IQvia, Ciox, Change Healthcare, and even IBM Watson Health power much of the transactional and analytic data creation. None of these companies, on a revenue basis, amount to even 5 percent of the size of the big five tech companies or, even when consistently profitable, garner similar valuations. On occasion HCIT companies such as Veeva, Teledoc, and Livongo become high-multiple public companies and drive investor headlines based on high growth and innovation. Rarely do any of the established HCIT companies, the ones that best understand the intricacies of the healthcare system, get acquired by the largest technology companies. This is presumably due, in part, to growth rates that are slower than those of Silicon Valley leaders. It's also due to concerns about getting tangled up with sensitive data. By contrast, early-stage companies in healthcare that are small enough to put up impressive growth numbers regularly get gobbled up by both the tech giants and the healthcare incumbents.

So the current landscape has very large tech companies who regularly talk about the importance of healthcare but barely play in the industry; significant incumbent organizations that are regulated as to their profitability and innovate within those constraints; and smaller but highly capable HCIT players who are asymmetrically small as compared to the other two types of entities.

Abundant Data Is Not Enough

When I think about the intersection of the incumbent healthcare industry and the high-tech sector, I am aware that the most overused cliché common to both is the concept that the "data" these organizations hold is the most valuable asset in the world. Data is either collected though input, produced though transactions, or derived from analysis of other data. Data becomes most valuable when it gets applied to solve a perplexing and massive problem. This means the real value is created when software algorithms (instructions), whether conventional, AI, or machine learning, act upon that data. The greatest value high-tech companies can provide is not in the data they develop and store but by partnering their innovation, talent, and capital investment capabilities to solve healthcare's difficult challenges. But high IQs and capital do not produce an understanding of the healthcare system. And healthcare is not broadly solvable through a mobile app.

> *The greatest value high-tech companies can provide is not in the data they develop and store but by partnering their innovation, talent, and capital investment capabilities to solve healthcare's difficult challenges.*

My prior book, *The Healthcare Cure*, spent considerable time detailing the variety of challenges we face in the healthcare industry and deciphering how it came to be the way it is today. From the opening pages of this book, the "grand" problem of healthcare is this: How can we achieve the greatest healthcare value—for a person or population—by getting the highest health status at the lowest total input cost? And of course, we have spent many pages discussing the two major types of inputs: clinical care and daily living. The size of big technology companies like Google or Apple or IBM offers no inherent uniqueness to solve this problem. They may be slightly advantaged because they are large employers and have the perspective of paying large amounts to insure their employees. They face the same impediments and reality barriers that all companies face in terms of data privacy and security issues. And they encounter the same difficulty everyone has when trying to understand how the healthcare system works today or how to understand the inertial forces that must be disrupted in order to promote meaningful change.

The pace of change in applying information technology to healthcare has long been criticized as exceedingly slow. This perceived slowness is a direct result of just how complicated, intertwined, and vast the industry is. On the one hand, it's an industry where Anthem or CVS-Aetna could not provide a full product were it not for the R&D and products of a Pfizer or Bristol-Myers Squibb. And retail pharmacies and hospitals could not exist without your HMO or PPO reimbursing them for the products and services you obtain. On the other hand, the scale of the industry is nearly unimaginable, as is the size of some of its biggest players, like the quarter-trillion-dollar United Health Group. Not long ago, Amazon, J. P. Morgan, and Berkshire Hathaway announced a new collaborative health venture they have named Haven. Even though these three entities have combined revenues roughly three times the size of United Health Group, the reality is that even when you put the roughly 1.5 million employees and the healthcare spend of these three corporations together, they would represent but a small commercial health plan. The largest nongovernment employer, Walmart, has over two million employees, and they have also spent many years and assembled great teams to make a bigger impact in healthcare. The point is, even these impressive organizations, who have great talent and the desire to change healthcare, are challenged to move the needle, but it's good that they're trying. Perhaps they would do so faster if their focus went beyond clinical care at a lower cost to holistic consumer health optimization.

Healthcare Has More Variables Than a Driverless Car

One way to think about the complications involved with change in healthcare is to consider a comparison to the development of self-driving cars, a nascent industry that has its roots in a partnership between auto manufacturers and data applications and software systems developed by the software engineers of Silicon Valley. The topic spent several months as daily headline news. Now, much more quietly, we are seeing and hearing stories of implementation delays, accidents, and legal standoffs. Self-driving technology is no easy task to master and is moving slower from concept to reality than most predicted. I don't wish to reduce the complexity of developing a fully functioning, safe, real-time driverless system or the immense data needed to drive a single vehicle, let alone millions. Yet for all the data required to maneuver a car in the dynamic environment of mixed modes of transportation—other vehicles, light rail trains, pedestrians, bicyclists, and so on—not only does the driverless car benefit from traffic that moves in a two-dimensional plane, but there is nowhere near the number of variables present in the data introduced to its system when compared with any given healthcare encounter. In simpler terms, almost anybody can drive; it's a little tougher to be a doctor, or a pharmacist, or a health plan administrator. Addressing a person's total healthcare needs across benefits and care entails all the complex, and individualized, considerations we have discussed in this book, utilizing vast volumes of biological data and seemingly limitless daily living variables.

Perhaps with biology as our model, we may well have created a nearly comparable level of complexity with the structure of the US healthcare system. Scanning the interconnectedness of healthcare entities required to complete any clinical care transaction can look a lot like a map of a human's central nervous system. Not only are there many more types of data inputs, but a wrong decision in someone's healthcare can also regularly have a far more profound impact. To put it simply, solving the problems of healthcare are infinitely more complicated than making a car not run into things. Placing enough sensors on a car to provide sufficient data for decision-making is easy compared to actually maneuvering that car in the ever-changing environment that is traffic. And while we can certainly place sensors on a person to monitor physical health data, a human is always going to be multidimensional. Both sides of this analogy—self-driving vehicles and healthcare—offer clear insight for why the data itself is not valuable; rather, it is the application of data that matters.

The good news is that Silicon Valley is far better positioned to assist with problem solving in the larger vision of optimizing people's health along the lines of daily living and social determinants than it is in aiding data use for treating clinical issues. Why? Because it already possesses far more data about where and how we live than what happens at our pharmacist or doctor's office. But Silicon Valley has shown scant interest in improving the health of the total population, despite inserting itself into healthcare circles from early in its inception. The companies we associate with Silicon Valley have experienced a great deal of success in getting information in front of people through advertising, causing them to click and buy things. Yet there couldn't be more of a double-edged sword than putting resources in front of people related to their health that are not helpful. Just as those in clinical care can lower an individual's health while costing the system a lot of money by providing unnecessary procedures or medication, putting programs and resources in front of consumers that are not evidence based and are not appropriate for improving health status can be just as harmful. Indeed, if clinical care accounts for only 30 percent of our total health, the potential to harm individuals through the misapplication of data and information technology regarding our daily living is far greater.

Of course, while the harm from misapplication can be greater in the 70 percent of what drives our health status, the potential impact for improving our health can be greater as well. Exponentially so. Yet, ironically, in the past Microsoft, Apple, Google, Oracle, and others have focused nearly all their attention on bringing new or applying existing technology toward electronic health records or clinical monitoring and interventions. Because, as we have been examining throughout the book, the information placed in such records by clinical providers or produced by sensors largely fails to connect to the benefit plans or social determinants of consumers, this data is largely irrelevant to consumers. As a result the information sources that have been the focus of attempts to intervene by Silicon Valley have had very little economic benefit or health benefit, thus far, for the consumer.

NOT JUST IN SICKNESS ... BUT ALSO IN HEALTH

Just as past dabbling in healthcare undertaken by high-tech companies has produced little value to the consumer, it mostly has been developed for reasons that aren't terribly helpful to the consumer. Rather than taking a holistic view of consumer's health, the motivation for developing new technology has been mostly to increase profits within existing business models. For example, much of the movement toward assisting in the development of medical health records was driven by a desire to sell more devices. When mobile phone manufacturers started embedding sensors that could help people track their exercise, monitor their sleep, or register their heart rate, the thought was that consumers would attribute a higher value to the device because of the sensors. That perception of value can drive more sales or seem to justify new products like smartwatches. And while it may be true that people will buy more devices with more sensors, the way the data from these sensors is applied is the more relevant point. Few have enough knowledge on their own to make use of the data such trackers have provided. If consumers can't share such data with their clinical providers and have that data assist them in making health decisions, then it's just binary information stored in electronic files. Sam may have paid big bucks for his Apple Watch, but mostly he uses it to track his fantasy football league. He certainly isn't sharing its wealth of lifestyle information with his doctor, and his doctor isn't using the information during the visit. If you don't have a holistic view of all of the things that a consumer might need to sustain their best and highest health, and if you're not putting a personalized set of resources before them that's relevant based on their benefit plan, their vocation, their social determinants, and their real social support system, then you're not really solving the problem.

Should we expect anything different? For all the very real brilliance of superbly talented data scientists and software engineers, they don't possess the background knowledge of how the healthcare system works. Why would they? Learning the intricacies of the healthcare system will take even very smart people many years of focused study and traditional experience. And as I mentioned, Silicon Valley tends not to absorb or integrate with the scaled HCIT companies. As a result, these highly capitalized, highly talented corporations actually have no real advantage for solving the healthcare affordability challenge or the healthcare access problem. After all, they are distracted by the fact that they've got top-line growth to produce and money to make from your consumer data. During the COVID-19 pandemic, most of these companies increased sales, profits, and stock value while infected people died and the rest of the population gained weight and became less mentally and physically resilient.

For all their relative inexperience with the complexities of the healthcare system, tech companies are further restricted by focusing nearly all the attention they do bring to the topic on clinical care, which is the one aspect of the larger system that we're already pretty good at managing effectively. I mentioned the recently formed entity, Haven, earlier. Haven may actually be able to accomplish a lot of good for its participants, getting employees access to the sickcare resources they need in a timely way and at a good price, but its focus is almost exclusive to these clinical resources. As a result, no matter how well designed this partnership proves in terms of its ability to work with clinical care providers, insurers, and others, they risk not addressing the larger problem and will have restricted themselves to a focus on what drives only 30 percent of their employees' health.

How Can Silicon Valley Help Healthcare?

How can Silicon Valley really help? First, they can recognize what the sickcare system has failed to do: that focusing on what drives only 30 percent of people's overall health is inherently restrictive in solving the problem. Next, they can stop assuming that the people who have been working in healthcare information technology and the incumbent healthcare system lack talent or skill. When applying some of the technologies Silicon Valley is best at producing, things like machine learning and AI, they have to recognize that anything they produce is bounded by human intelligence. If humans don't have a fulsome algorithm or learning model to apply, all the data in the world will be of little consequence. Silicon Valley's role can be asking data scientists to understand and develop evidence bases for how daily living correlates to health. Data that gets picked up through social media feeds, purchasing habits, and motion and biologic sensors need to be studied and understood so that more complex machine learning models identifying the variables that drive health and encourage receptivity to lifestyle change can be developed. We need data analysis capable of recognizing what resources are available to individuals and whether those individuals are in positions that allow them to make change possible given their social determinants. This will require data well beyond what is currently gathered in clinical settings and that is linked to people's benefit plans and to environmental and social factors.

To accomplish such ends, companies with technological expertise will have to form partnerships with those who possess healthcare expertise and then adopt a holistic vision of the healthcare system. That will mean going well beyond partnering with and employing doctors, which is currently how they tend to initiate massive investments in healthcare IT. Doctors understand how data can be applied for the diagnosis and treatment of patients, and some can extrapolate data for treating a population, but there are many other aspects of the larger healthcare system in which they lack expertise. As I've said before, in the expansive and complicated world of healthcare, its various segments seldom understand how others operate. Partnering with doctors, while a useful first step, is at least 70 percent insufficient.

When it comes to helping contribute to healthcare solutions, perhaps the greatest hurdle of all for Silicon Valley is to set aside its current profit model and the embedded hubris of presumed superiority in data and software technology, at least for a while, and sincerely think about how to increase the health and well-being of people systematically. In part, they should take more interest in understanding the challenges faced and overcome by the HCIT players who have been solving the healthcare riddle for years and decades. This is, of course, no small request. The probable level of investment to really get their hands dirty, and the potential challenges of integrating cultures of business-to-consumer technologists with enterprise-level thinkers who have the experience to piece together the messiness of healthcare, is immense. Add in the reality that the capital market environment punishes companies for slowdowns in growth or profit, and it's a really huge commitment. We certainly don't have to stand against corporate profits—in healthcare or in data and software technology—but improving the health of people is more impactful and more complicated than what can be reflected short term in the columns of a profit/loss statement. I am calling for partnerships between Silicon Valley and the healthcare industry to hold the improvement of

> *I am calling for partnerships between Silicon Valley and the healthcare industry to hold the improvement of people's total health and well-being as their first mission.*

people's total health and well-being as their first mission. Doing so can extend healthier and more fulfilling lives. And it can be done while still turning a tidy profit.

To close this chapter, let's return to our encyclopedic hardware store owner from chapter 5. While envisioning the needs of a systematic framework that incorporates daily living and social determinants, I reminded you how impossible it is to scale the personalized attention and knowledge base our hardware store owner represents. Now, assume that owner is your neighbor, your local small businessperson. You wouldn't wish to deny such a valuable asset to your town a profit, would you? Quite the opposite. You'd want to bring your business to the store. Of course, you're not patronizing the hardware store with a mind to providing it profit; rather, you perceive value in the goods and services you receive there. If that weren't the case, you'd go somewhere else. With our mythical store owner, you don't just get the material you need in a manner that makes it easy to find, but you also receive expert advice at putting it to work. As a result of that perceived value, you're happy to spend your money within his store.

More important still, don't forget the biggest reason I introduced this analogy in the first place: Since we don't have cloning of humans available to us, such a business model is impossible to scale without the aid of technology. We need the value Silicon Valley can bring to healthcare, but we've got to realize that its real value is in combining knowledgeable human capital that exists beyond its culture with the innovative approaches to problem solving its people can offer. At risk of redundancy, the value high tech can provide is not in the data but rather in applying the data based on knowledge of how the healthcare industry actually functions. And when we hear about the applications of machine learning and artificial intelligence, I trust that you can see how a systematic and holistic framework could make for amazing outcomes for individuals and society. Technology alone will not solve the healthcare problem. However, applied technology, motivated first and foremost by the goal of helping everyone take actions to achieve and sustain their highest health status, can.

Part V: From This Day Forward

Working Together to Achieve Health Optimization

CHAPTER 10

HEALTH OPTIMIZATION IS COMMON SENSE AND POLITICAL COMMON GROUND

In this age of political tribalism, in which politicians can't seem to agree on anything, I may seem like an outlier—or worse—when I suggest that there can be widespread agreement on both sides of the aisle when it comes to the ideas outlined in this book. Now, I know that agreement may seem out of fashion in the current political climate, but my belief that it can be achieved goes well beyond my enthusiasm for the topic. I'm not really interested in political labels generally. Rather, I see the world as a series of problems to solve. And when it comes to healthcare, I emphasize practicality and meaning-ful improvement in people's total health and well-being while being cost efficient. Neither emphasis area is a political construct. As I have advocated throughout this book, systematic frameworks and applied information technology can accelerate the improvement of people's health. While representing the conjoined interests of healthcare and IT, I've spent plenty of time speaking with members of Congress and policy makers from both parties about just how we might use the approaches outlined in this book to solve the great American problem of making high-quality holistic care available to all. Those conversations have only solidified my belief that there's more common ground than the heated rhetoric of political campaigns or the pot stirring of media in search of viewership might suggest.

Looking for Agreement

So, let's talk about what just about everybody already agrees on.

First, there's certainly agreement that the United States suffers an *affordability crisis* in healthcare. We can all acknowledge that for far too many people, the cost of gaining access to clinical care creates a major financial challenge. Often these financial challenges extend across the benefits framework we have spoken about at length—Medicaid, Medicare, Tricare, VA, and commercial insurance, whether the latter is provided through employers or the exchange programs established by the ACA. We readily anticipate affordability issues for some of these segments because of the lower income levels and higher health needs of many of the people they represent, but we would be negligent if we did not acknowledge deficiencies in affordability where we might least expect it. For example, many individuals who work for small businesses, are self-employed, or are part of the "gig economy" struggle to find healthcare coverage on insurance exchanges that does not take up a large percentage of their income. This has been well documented in the media. The mythology of ready access to health insurance coverage became all too real during the coronavirus crisis of 2020.

When it comes to affordability, we all recognize that the cost of health insurance, no matter the segment, continues to escalate year by year faster than most other costs in our lives. In the most recent year for which we have data, 2018, the average increase in subsidies paid was $201 per insured individual or family.[28] In an age of high-deductible plans and escalating sickcare costs, those served by employer-purchased plans can struggle with healthcare budgets as well. According to the National Conference of State Legislatures, "In 2018 the average annual premium for employer-based family coverage rose five percent to $19,616; for single coverage, premiums rose three percent to $6,896. Covered workers contributed eighteen percent of the cost for single coverage and twenty-nine percent of the cost for family coverage, on average, with considerable variation across firms."[29] Seniors with conventional Medicare coverage who have the financial means to do so frequently buy Medicare supplemental coverage through private insurers to help offset the rising costs of needed care or pharmaceuticals, as they see the same pattern of increasing costs. For consumers, political party affiliation doesn't determine your view on healthcare nearly as much as your benefit type does, and virtually all beneficiaries regardless of benefit type or income level are of the mind, probably rightfully, that finding affordable, quality care continues to become increasingly difficult.

Another thing that there's general political agreement on is support of the concept known as *managed care*. Managed care, at its core, provides guidelines to deliver resources within a budget for a population, while providing individuals with the most effective care for a given condition or illness. It also establishes health benefit plan rules for what services and goods can be provided by which type of provider, in which setting, and at what cost. Recall that there are non-managed care programs for both Medicare and Medicaid. However, nearly three-quarters of Medicaid beneficiaries are in managed care programs, and managed Medicare, known as Medicare Advantage, represents well over a third of the senior population and is growing rapidly. In commercial insurance, over 95 percent of beneficiaries are in managed care plans.[30] I was fortunate in my career to be a health plan executive involved in the early formation of both commercial managed care and Medicare Advantage and to then build information technology organizations that powered managed care into the mainstream. If you have an accounting and analytical mind, managed care plans allow you to classify and budget expenses into categories like primary care, specialty care, emergency care, outpatient care, inpatient hospital care, prescription drugs, specialty pharma, and medical equipment and supplies—among dozens of others. These essentially are organizational categories for resource planning necessary to manage the clinical care for a population. When you proactively apply these categories and use data and information to predict and move people toward the right resources, managed care ascends to the concept of population health management, which is the current in-vogue term. No matter the terminology used, population health management is managed care. And managed care takes us all the way back to our initial equation, where for every dollar spent on healthcare, the intention is to create efficiency for the set of input costs in the denominator:

$$H_v = \frac{\textit{Health Status (person or population)}}{\textit{Clinical Care ("omics")} + \textit{Daily Living (SDoH)}}$$

Yet despite this agreement, very few legislators or governmental agencies understand the equation as I've written it. They tend to incessantly argue about only the access to the clinical care component, and they treat issues of social determinants impacting daily living as divisive political fodder. While Republicans and Democrats alike may fail to understand the unifying equation, at least when it comes to clinical care, most agree that we need the framework of managed care to help make certain people can receive efficacious, evidence-based care from reputable providers. Starting from that agreement is our best hope to help our representatives in government embrace an expanded vision of what healthcare includes and the larger scope of health improvement resources that belong in the equation's denominator.

A third source of agreement that is nonpartisan, despite a lot of suggestions otherwise and a good deal of disagreement on the details, is this: *Access to basic healthcare is a fundamental right.* Liberal or conservative, most agree that there needs to be some sort of essential health safety net for all citizens of the United States. The major sticking point that leads to a great deal of contention is the question, Does such a safety net literally apply only to "citizens"? As a result, the basic philosophical belief in healthcare as a right becomes bogged down in a separate debate over whether such rights extend to people no matter their immigration status. Step over these citizenship hurdles, and I think you will have a hard time finding any member of Congress who would not advocate that people deserve access to care.

> *A third source of agreement that is nonpartisan, despite a lot of suggestions otherwise and a good deal of disagreement on the details, is this: Access to basic healthcare is a fundamental right.*

Despite this general agreement, however, a point of contention arises in varying interpretations or definitions of what qualifies as "basic healthcare." It's a complex topic that I've spent years addressing, but suffice it to say that if you remove politics, it takes us back to our BMW versus Kia analogy. A well-engineered, high-quality solution does not necessarily have to be so expensive and might even be more reliable for most. As new medical and surgical procedures are developed and new pharmaceuticals and genetic engineering approaches are discovered, some wonder if everyone should have access to the most leading-edge treatments available regardless of their cost or relative efficacy. Such questions are best managed within the structures of the health benefit plan categories we discussed in chapter 3, where we gained an understanding that "it's the benefits, stupid." With well-developed skills to differentiate moral high ground across the political spectrum, the politicians grab this tiger by the tail and bite their opponents.

The obvious separators of the parties generally lead us back to the view of benefits available for women's reproductive health, low-income populations and—to turn a phrase—benefits for those who don't have benefits. If we didn't have issues of women's reproductive rights, the causes and effects of socioeconomic inequality, and immigration to argue about, how would the media spend its time? My apolitical view is that applying the unifying equation is the best way to knock down socioeconomic disparities by personalizing daily living support resources with an understanding of social determinants. Beyond the political dividers, however, the topic can get quite complicated and nuanced. For example, let's say there is a new cancer treatment—one that is expensive and is resource intensive—that might benefit Fred's wife. Even the manufacturer says it is likely to extend life by an average of ninety days. Does her advanced age and dementia make her a "lesser" candidate for the treatment? Does her status as a taxpayer-funded Medicare recipient rather than a for-profit private commercial beneficiary alter how clinicians treat her condition? Does her ability or inability to pay for a given percentage of her treatment alter how we see her right to access? Do we believe that there are circumstances where one individual or family should be required to pay more than another? We speculate on such matters in part because we realize the exorbitant costs often associated with state-of-the-art treatments and recognize they can't realistically be applied to everyone. We look at other countries that provide more socialized approaches to healthcare and observe that "free" care necessarily also often means no-frills care or wait-in-line care. And if those people want to cut the line, they pay out-of-pocket. These discussions are generally rational, until it affects you or someone you love. Being eighty-five years old seems far away until your parent is eighty-four, or even more poignantly, when you are eighty-three. Likewise, the concept of participating in a clinical trial or cutting-edge treatment is an interesting scientific thought (which most people do not understand) until the subject is a mother with three young children, or a child, or a person hit with a pandemic virus like COVID-19. We all recognize that sometimes more advanced treatments may not be affordable, but we also see that connecting individuals from very different benefit populations to resources with a consistent set of values is important.

Building a Health Safety Net

Rather than getting bogged down in the political arguments, we need to focus on the broader acceptance that we must build a better health safety net, one that can be strengthened by digital fibers and one that can be orchestrated based on the well-established principles of managed care. Again, politicians of both parties not only agree that we need managed care but also that using information technology to create healthier people and healthier populations is a good idea. There is also agreement that data privacy that is accordant

> *We must build a better health safety net, one that can be strengthened by digital fibers and one that can be orchestrated based on the well-established principles of managed care.*

with sensitive healthcare issues should be ensured and enforced. And recently a great deal of common sense was exhibited by politicians in relaxing difficult-to-administer privacy regulations that would have slowed the response to COVID-19 and also made it more difficult for consumers to obtain healthcare services on a virtual basis. Once we go beyond the application of electronic health records—something nearly all politicians were quick to see as beneficial—there's little understanding of or agreement on how other types of administrative or consumer data could or should be applied. Yet this is the area of greatest opportunity for further agreement because, once it has been demonstrated, as this book has tried to do, nearly every educated person, regardless of their party, understands that the actions that drive the highest health and well-being in individuals and populations go far beyond the realm of our current sickcare benefits system.

If you take a systematic approach and look around the rest of the world, a very interesting pattern develops. In countries that most Americans would deem "socialist"—think of countries like Sweden or the Netherlands, for example—social spending on things like housing, education, food (i.e., the social determinants) are much higher than in the United States as a percentage of gross national product (GDP), but healthcare spending is lower. In 2017 the United States spent $10,224 per capita on healthcare compared to $5,511 in Sweden. This pattern holds equally true for other wealthy, industrialized countries such as Germany, the United Kingdom, and Canada. Indeed, if you focus only on healthcare spending for a moment, a 2017 study by the Kaiser Family Foundation determined that other wealthy countries consistently spend about half of what the United States does, averaging $5,280 per capita.[31] Now factor in some of the items that might fall into our equation's denominator. Another wealthy, industrialized country, France, is quite representative of a number of other nations in this regard. France spends over 30 percent of its GDP on public social programs such as those that provide unemployment aid, housing assistance, and benefits to the aged, children, and the disabled. By comparison, the United States spends less than 20 percent of its GDP on similar programs. But if you add medical expenditures and this other social spending together, guess what? The spending is pretty close.[32] At the end of the day we're in somewhat of a closed loop equation. The total dollars spent on these two categories of public support programs are finite within a given annual budget for any country. Right now, we've essentially created a US belief system that these two sets of expenditures represent two pieces of a GDP pie. This book argues that if we really want to measure what contributes to total health, clinical care and daily living resources must be considered in total.

Because of information technology and its virtualization and localization programming capabilities, resources can be delivered with personalized precision at great scale regardless of location, resulting in the opportunity for much lower-cost inputs for supporting daily living. Expanding the thinking of politicians on the use of data and information technology is directly connected to my earlier point about the reality that we have categorized people by their benefit plans. By nature politicians are programmed to think in terms of what their constituents want from them or, more accurately, what politicians *perceive* to be the interests of the voting blocs that elect them. If a politician's voting district has a significant percentage of low-income Medicaid beneficiaries who want access to basic clinical healthcare services but often encounter difficulty accessing care, then talking about resources to help manage stress, financial and career planning, or building supportive personal relationships may not necessarily be a hot political topic. Ensuring that there are accessible clinics and pharmacies is a much simpler topic. And yet, ironically, the Medicaid population would benefit the most from having access to nonclinical health improvement resources that directly affect the realities of their daily lives, resources to help them cope with challenges that are so heavily impacted by SDoH.

There may be numerous diabetes management programs that would greatly benefit Sarah, but if they require her to leave her immediate neighborhood, are presented in an unsafe environment, or aren't offered during hours when she has access to childcare, she's not going to see their value. She certainly won't see value when compared to what seems the immediate need of obtaining insulin or getting her asthmatic daughter to an emergency room. If Sarah struggles to see the benefits as applied to her own life, then you can bet the politician representing her district either can't see such benefits or believes he or she could never "sell" the Sarahs who voted them into office on why such programs are valuable. Similarly, programs to educate Sarah on nutrition and incent her toward healthy eating are not as immediately understandable in their benefit as providing funding to support food kitchens in her district. Similarly, it's hard to argue that shelters for people in abusive relationships or for those dependent on unhealthy substances are vital as compared to programs to build healthy relationships or develop mental resiliency. Not unlike the prior discussion on cutting-edge clinical treatments, the immediacy of a problem trumps all when you are experiencing it. But back to the concept of quality—what if 90 percent of the energy of auto manufacturers went into how to better complete repairs versus designing and engineering products that are far less likely to break? The former would make for "unhealthy" automobiles.

Just like quality in manufacturing, the first step is helping educate politicians on why a broader vision of healthcare—beyond sickcare— can make their constituents' lives better *and* save money. If we fail to accomplish such education, then we risk falling into the traps so frequently set because of the political divide that inaccurately is applied to discussions of healthcare reform. Politicians who occupy a deeply divided body politic tend to want to treat healthcare policy as yet another subject for division, when in fact, as we've seen, there is a good deal of agreement. In my experience as a leader, you have to have a framework that is understandable to overcome the current political climate's hyperfocus on specific areas of disagreement. Without a framework—for example, most people agree that more jobs and a growing economy are good things—politicians who are not necessarily experts on the healthcare system in total are bound to succumb to the desires of lobbyists or false presentations of others' positions.

> *Politicians who occupy a deeply divided body politic tend to want to treat healthcare policy as yet another subject for division, when in fact, as we've seen, there is a good deal of agreement.*

And just like the politicians elected to represent us, voting populations may misinterpret factual information or fall victim to political rhetoric directed at our sensitivities. We've seen examples where political interests pander to some of seniors' generational biases. For example, many seniors, like Fred and his wife, grew up within social constructs about authority that made them swift to place blind trust in their doctors. Sam may be quick (too quick, perhaps) to turn to Google for answers to his medical questions, and Sarah—try as she might—may not even be able to realistically establish a relationship with a primary physician. Where Fred, Sam, and Sarah may be most united is in their distrust of the effectiveness of politicians, holding cynical visions of their motivations.

I could give numerous examples of confusing, divisive, and inaccurate statements on healthcare from both political parties, but this is not a book about politics ... and hundreds of countervailing wrongs don't make a right. The many occurrences of politicians, with the help of the media, getting voters to accept nonfactual information underlies something that has been at the heart of this book: Altering our nation's approach to move from sickcare to health optimization—not just in sickness ... but also in health—needs to be simplified into a framework that most people can understand. Fox News and CNN don't put on guests who debate whether jobs and economic growth are good things; rather, they endlessly debate who is responsible (or to blame) for the positive or negative growth of each. Can you imagine a real debate as to *whether* the health of a person or any group of people is impacted by both clinical care *plus* the things people do in their daily lives, and whether those daily things are impacted by education, income, environmental safety, and other factors that make up people's lives? Yes, there could be endless debate as to how to impact those social determinants, what is the individual versus governmental and societal responsibility, and who gets the credit or blame—but there would still be a framework of agreement. My hopes were heightened that agreeable frameworks are possible when on June 5, 2020, as many parts of the nation were coping with what it meant to "get back to work" after widescale shutdowns in response to a pandemic, a jobs report was released that surprised both Democrats and Republicans. This report, which indicated that nearly ten million more people had returned to work than had been forecast, was disseminated in what appeared to be a factual way.[33] The same factuality is true of GDP reporting. And the same, unfortunately, is true when reporting COVID-19 deaths. My point is this: If people can agree on a framework and something can be measured—even if political parties want to argue the why and whether a trend is sustainable—there is a chance to bring people together.

Accuracy when discussing something as complicated as healthcare is essential. Accuracy when discussing a vision of healthcare that intertwines—as it should—all the elements of our daily lives becomes even more difficult. Furthermore, as we discussed in chapter 8, when discussing privacy concerns and healthcare, people are particularly sensitive to matters that affect them at a personal level. For most, little seems more personal than their health and their ability to access and pay for the things that can keep them healthy. Once we expand the purview of healthcare to include the daily living multiplier of social determinants in our unifying equation's denominator, there's even greater room for policy makers to overstep knowingly or to fall into blind traps set by lobbyists and special interest groups.

The Promise of Political Parties Acting on Common Agreement

There is a vital counterbalance opportunity for political divisiveness—nothing less than an opportunity to transform hundreds of millions of lives for the better. What is at stake is so important that we must remind politicians to turn away from their lesser instincts to partake in partisan quibbles and focus instead on the widespread points of agreement about healthcare I have outlined in this chapter. We saw firsthand the powerful and positive impact of

> There is a vital counterbalance opportunity for political divisiveness—nothing less than an opportunity to transform hundreds of millions of lives for the better.

bipartisan efforts on our nation with economic stimulus to offset the crushing economic impact of COVID-19 shutdowns. We are living in an era of transforming expectations about health, as benefit plan designs are shifting significantly toward being proactive and supporting total well-being. Organizations from labor unions to corporations to benefit providers are recognizing that they should be looking for an enriched sense of benefits that helps people learn how to manage those other aspects of their lives that affect health status. In order to contend in a competitive skilled labor market, employers are far more likely to provide additional health coaching, health education, wellness activities, and access to fitness programs. Such offerings parallel movements for greater work location and scheduling flexibility as employers increasingly have to think about the reality that their workers are not necessarily going to keep regular hours or predominantly work in an employer-provided office environment. Managed Medicaid programs continue to increase the nature and breadth of their offerings. Many Medicare Advantage plans not only extend traditional Medicare benefits to vision and dental care, but they also often include fitness and nutrition benefits, condition management support, and even transportation assistance.

And while there remains much that is unclear about the future of the political hot potato of the Affordable Care Act (a.k.a. Obamacare), there certainly are aspects of it, like extending family plan availability until age twenty-six and removing denial of insurance for preexisting conditions, that have overwhelming and bipartisan support among voters. There is essentially a unanimous understanding that traditional sickcare is not likely to get any less expensive. It takes no crystal ball to recognize that we will continue to see more advanced treatment options, more sophisticated, targeted medicines, and breakthrough procedures using the power of gene therapy. This is all a way to reinforce that we are at the brink of a point where Republicans and Democrats alike can see that driving health optimization and proactively working to flatten the morbidity curve for as long as possible is in the best interest of everyone. It is long past time for all of us to recognize such a truth.

The right resources to the right person, delivered over the right channel at the right time—that's the formula to reduce the total cost of healthcare inputs relative to total health status. The things we've

> *The right resources to the right person, delivered over the right channel at the right time—that's the formula to reduce the total cost of healthcare inputs relative to total health status.*

discussed since the outset of this book when defining daily living—condition management, fitness, nutrition, and relationship management, to name just four—can be made more accessible and affordable with the proper use of information technology. Without cloning humans, we have a path to solve the hardware store owner dilemma.

For political expedience, we can label the systematic framework that I call *health optimization* with whatever term suits people's needs—holistic health care, total well-being, or even simply "improving the human condition." But it's certainly a construct that unites those of differing political persuasions precisely because it unites people across all economic and ethnic backgrounds. I have purposefully not told you anything about the political affiliations of Fred, María, Sarah, or Sam for one simple reason: It doesn't matter! They are of different ages, come from different backgrounds, and no doubt have differing beliefs about politics. All four have different benefit plans, different health conditions, different social determinants, and different genetics.

But they are united, like we all are, in their desire to be the healthiest versions of themselves.

The approach in this book advocates for the fact that healthcare is not a partisan issue and it is long past time we stopped treating it as if it were. If we put more energy into distribution of health improvement resources that can be targeted using improved data analytics, delivered digitally or less expensively scaled locally using information technology, then we're *all* better off. The nation's better off. And, frankly, we can pivot from the complex benefits of the US healthcare system and use the data and software information technology strengths of the United States to help make the world better off!

CHAPTER 11

CREATING INTELLIGENT ECOSYSTEMS FOR OPTIMIZED HEALTH AND TOTAL WELL-BEING

At the outset of this book, I discussed my personal dependence on clinical care for the treatment of my own chronic condition and my appreciation for those medical professionals who have been so important to my life and my health. Quite literally, without the ability to access such care, I wouldn't be in the circumstance—alive, that is—to write this book. While I steadfastly believe that the healthcare industry is overly skewed toward sickness, everything I have proposed in this book is built on a recognition that, despite the incompleteness of the larger system, the United States generally excels at providing outstanding clinical care for the majority of people the majority of the time. And the coronavirus pandemic of 2020, even with its frightening, poignant exposure of specific weaknesses in the sickcare system, clearly showed that our medical professionals and clinical supply chain can ultimately rise to the occasion.

Few to One to Many

What is novel about the system this book is advancing is the opportunity for coordination *among three different types* of entities—the incumbent healthcare enterprises (sponsors), consumers, and health improvement resources (point solutions). I call this systems approach *few to one to many*. I do so because in my core I am quite literally a techno-geek and a nerd or, less pejoratively, a systems analyst and an accountant. From a data design perspective, this complex relationship of few to one to many is an accurate description of the way technologists need to approach the problem. I can assure you that it's a very complex problem, or it would have long ago been solved. If innovation must be steeped in tradition, then we cannot solve the problem of achieving the unifying equation without deeply understanding and respecting the situation we are in. We can't start with a blank piece of paper that doesn't acknowledge the existence of the incumbent players who comprise the $3.5 trillion system today: health plans, employers, health service providers, pharmacies, and health-related not-for-profit community organizations. I call these the "few" because every consumer, including you and me, has a handful of relationships at any given time with these entities. For example, María has a health plan, an employer, a set of medical providers, a favorite pharmacy, and an affiliation with a nonprofit entity that helps her support her parents. In other words, from a data standpoint, we can associate María with a manageable number of specific incumbent entities. For simplification, I call these entities *sponsors* because in addition to selling what they sell, they all have potential interest in paying for both the programs and incentives to partner María with the "many." The *many*, unlike the few, is a nearly endless list of potential health improvement resources that I simply call *point solutions*. You know what point solutions are even if you don't call them by that name. These point solutions include fitness, nutrition, disease and condition management, stress, sleep, resilience, financial planning, relationship management, and the like. Sometimes they are mobile apps; sometimes they are goods and services; sometimes they are human-human or computer-human interactions. Did I mention that there are *many* such solutions? An assembly of these point solutions put together by a sponsor is a health improvement resource ecosystem. A specific combination of these point solutions that are assembled in a personalized way for a consumer is an *intelligent health improvement resource ecosystem.*

The graphic depiction below illustrates a way to envision the few to one to many relationships without naming any specific entities.

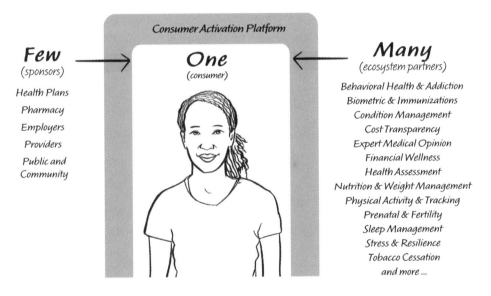

You've probably already figured out that the intelligent ecosystem is comprised of the very resources we've been discussing, the ones that support a consumer in daily living. Largely, the conveyance and management of clinical care comes through the incumbents on the left of the figure above. Similarly, the conveyance of daily living support comes through the point solutions on the right. In today's world, all conveyances can be physical, virtual (i.e., telehealth), digital, or a hybrid of all three. Give Sarah, Fred, María, or Sam the right combination, and you will have happier and healthier consumers at lower costs. And voilà—in the eleventh chapter we've now closed the loop of how to support the unifying equation from a systems point of view. With this in mind, let's look once again at our unifying equation:

$$H_V = \frac{\text{Health Status (person or population)}}{\text{Clinical Care ("omics") + Daily Living (SDoH)}}$$

At this point, you might be thinking that we are not paying enough attention to the clinical care aspects of the denominator. In other words, aren't the clinical resources surrounding a person part of their intelligent ecosystem too? Of course they are!

Let's break down the clinical care incumbents to better understand how intelligence must be a combination of clinical and daily living resources. Then we can look at some examples of partnerships that have already formed and that are having positive impacts on total health.

A major point throughout this book has been to expand our perspective on what affects our health. In a similar vein, when we look across those entities to which we traditionally turn to manage our health problems clinically, we have to remember to maintain a wide aperture. For example, when we think about clinical care health providers, we have to look beyond just our primary care physician, his or her staff, and all the specialists they might refer us to, and consider the importance of our dentist, our chiropractor, our physical therapist, the nutritionist, the psychological therapist, and even the acupuncturist or massage therapist we might use. Similarly, when we think about an institutional hospital, we must also consider all the arms of that hospital administrative unit, the urgent care centers they run, the outpatient surgical centers, the ambulatory clinics, infusion centers, labs, diagnostic imaging and testing centers, and rehabilitation clinics. If we consider our local pharmacy, we've really also got to think of the pharmacy benefit management company, which establishes the price and distribution of the medicines we need, and give some thought to the "big pharma" organizations that develop therapies we ingest. Again, we're talking incumbent players, and we could easily develop long lists of these clinical care entities and consider the functions each performs. But my simple challenge to you here is to think of these incumbents in the most broadly systematic and integrated way possible. If we don't, we fail to see all of the positive ecosystem partnerships that can form when we allow other players to join them at the table or the power of resources developed specifically with the consumer in mind.

The illustration below shows the traditional way we think about how the incumbent clinical care resources need to be built into an intelligent clinical ecosystem for consumers:

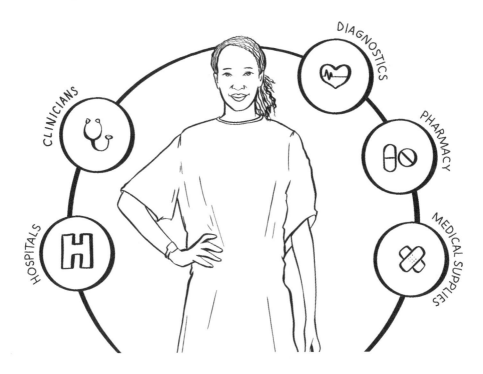

There are plenty of opportunities to improve the conveyance of a clinical ecosystem around consumers, and I don't mean to diminish the amount of innovation that could and should occur or downplay the probable 20 percent or greater efficiency (cost savings) that would be possible. However, as a reminder, even if a perfect clinical ecosystem were developed around each consumer, it would impact less than 30 percent of health status. While I support improving clinical efficiency to save a lot of money, it won't drive significantly higher health status. Remember that clinical care largely occurs as episodic and acute care, and we are striving for a system that recognizes that true optimal health includes the whole of a person and goes beyond traditional medical biometrics and the abatement of disease. There is a significant movement toward *integrative healthcare* that fuses Western and Eastern medical thinking in this regard. However, nothing in this book is intended to diminish the importance of clinical care nor advocate abandoning what we already do best in healthcare in this country. Indeed, we will not succeed in getting people to achieve their highest health status without clinical care experts of all varieties employing the most efficacious practices they have developed over time or in crisis. It's just that we need to do more.

Admittedly, it's easy to talk about taking a more expansive view but hard to implement it. I wrote an entire other book about how the traditional healthcare system works, and to be candid, most people who work in the industry today—or who opine on it—could not diagram out the relationships among the incumbent players. Think about all the moving pieces just in medical care: They include, of course, all the frontline clinical care providers working in small and large practices. They also include hospitals, pharmacies, the benefit plan providers, our employers, and government. If you can just keep track of those in regard to your and your family's situation, you are far ahead of most people.

But the vision we've discussed throughout this book means we also must "see" all those health improvement resources that fall outside those we reference when talking about traditional clinical care: media and social media organizations, search engine operators, gaming device companies, nutrition providers (grocery stores, restaurants, subscription meal services, etc.), and point solution providers of condition management (i.e., stress management, financial management, relationship management, behavioral health management, etc.). We must include all those agencies and organizations on which so many people are dependent for human services: community organizations that provide localized shelters, food kitchens, food pantries, job training, counseling services, and topical support groups. There are others, of course, but you get the picture. You might say, "Wow, this is about as complicated as life!" And you would be largely correct. But that doesn't prevent us from systematically creating intelligence around an individual. Let's take a look at an illustration of how we might picture daily support resources around an individual below:

One thing is clear—we must know quite a bit about a person to get them the right mix of health improvement resources. A second point of clarity is that the flow of data and information as the consumer interacts with these resources is immense. The challenge of assembling such an aspirational set of resources is that we must be able to apply information technology to keep track of the people and the possibilities. We've seen industries spend tens and hundreds of millions of dollars to develop information systems that use both traditional computing and artificial intelligence (or machine learning) to properly stock the aisles of Walmart, the fulfillment center aisles of Amazon, or the aisles of Ace Hardware. We've watched the retail industry, even across competitors, cooperate on what these categories are, giving them codes or numbers so that you know the difference between a box of cereal or a box of nails. But the truth is that as an industry healthcare has never really taken on the project of creating a "store" where every human being can enter, can provide the inputs about themselves, their health, their social determinants, their aspiration, their goals to come out with a suggestion list of how they can achieve their total health and well-being at the lowest possible cost. Understand that before such a dream can be realized, you have to have the information systems in place to support the dream. Walmart could never run with a manual inventory system. Amazon could never operate if you had to call up someone on the phone and have them explain to you all the items you might be able to buy. But remember, they both have the advantage of innovating off of many years of retail experience in which products were categorized and placed into aisles, whether physical or virtual.

Categorizing Point Solutions for Total Well-Being

Throughout this book I have been slipping in the term "total well-being" repeatedly without explaining the definition. In part, I did this because the term well-being is used so often today, I assumed it would not be distracting. The other reason, however, was to save a tidbit for the reader who is curious about my view on its meaning. Since this book is full of frameworks that support the codification of health optimization, as you might imagine I have a strong viewpoint on the concept of total well-being. If you search for a definition of the word *well-being* you will find various combinations of healthy, happy, prosperous, and joyful. When I express the achievement of optimal health and total well-being, I am expressly saying that the highest health status, even though health is impacted by social determinants, is not the ultimate systematic goal. The achievement of optimal health *and* total well-being is the status I would prefer for all individuals in our country and the billions around the globe. I realize it's a never-ending goal, and as I stated

> *The achievement of optimal health and total well-being is the status I would prefer for all individuals in our country and the billions around the globe.*

in the introduction, I have tried throughout my life to be innovative while respecting the traditions that have preceded me.

Several years ago I was fortunate to develop a professional and personal relationship with a leader at IBM named Dr. Kyu Rhee. Dr. Rhee, IBM's chief health officer, is a remarkably humble and accomplished man. He was very kind to tell me how much he appreciated my prior book, *The Healthcare Cure,* as we discussed how to transform an industry. As Welltok worked with IBM to implement their view of holistic health for IBM's employees on our consumer activation platform, Dr. Rhee introduced me to what they labeled *the five dimensions of health*. Recall from our earlier chapters that health improvement resources tend to show up for consumers in fragmented ways. But can they be assembled and personalized to really impact total well-being? Such a scenario isn't far-fetched at all. In fact, let's look at IBM's publicly available example, which begins to forecast a different kind of health future. Here, a large employer created a whole division that advocates the benefits of leading a balanced life by applying these five dimensions, as stated in IBM's "Culture of Health" documents:

- Physical—Healthy recipes, or new ways to get and stay active.

- Mind—Tools for reducing stress, improved cognition, and relieved anxiety are a few ways you can invest in your mental health.

- Financial—From retirement planning to investment tools and planning your future, these make life easier to manage.

- Social—Balance work and life with family and friends, build healthier relationships, or make new connections.

- Purpose—Align values with your life and work.[34]

Applying these dimensions and using their data application expertise, IBM then curates a rich set of resources, using the data science of personalization, to help match the right resources to the right person, all while respecting the privacy of those individuals. This example of a business-to-consumer ecosystem demonstrates the power of developing an expansive vision of health.

Having worked with IBM and many other organizations over the years at Welltok and in other contexts, it was one of the few times that I saw a framework that was—in short—right on point! With the aim of taming the cacophonous health improvement resources represented by the many, the framework for total well-being, with only a minor tweak to the prior list—and regardless of whether the benefit plan type is commercial (like IBM), Medicare, Medicaid, or the military—can be expressed as follows:

1. physical health

2. mental health

3. social health

4. financial health

5. purpose

Let's quickly walk through these.

Because *physical health* includes fitness, nutrition, condition management, and sleep management, we can start to think about what types of point solution resources you would line up in each of those categories that could then be matched or personalized to an individual. Of course, for most benefit plans, physical health resources are first construed to mean access to clinical resources that monitor standard biometrics and treat disease—that is, the medical, dental, and vision resource network available through a benefit plan.

When we think about *mental health*, just as IBM thinks about managing stress and improving cognition, you can include point solutions for building resilience, managing depression, alleviating boredom, coping with substance abuse, improving mental acuity, and the like.

When it comes to *social health* and relationships, people are, of course, highly divergent. Fred is married but obviously in a rapidly changing situation. Sam is single and possibly enjoying it or possibly trying to figure out the dating scene in a world where social norms are quite different than when Fred met his wife. Sarah, as a single mother, must seek support in relationships that are realistic for her situation and learn to carve time out so that she has some for herself. And María, who would seem to have the American Dream, might need some help to ensure that her long-standing and healthy relationship with her husband doesn't deteriorate now that the kids have moved out.

In the area of *financial health*, you can think about assembling basic financial literary resources—how to save, how to spend smartly, how to prepare for a future, whether it's paying for housing, education, weddings, retirement, and ... wait for it ... healthcare! And, although Sarah and Fred are very different and Sam is very young, each one of those individuals could be presented resources that are appropriate. Maybe Sarah is able to put savings into play with the extra change that rounds up to the nearest dollar in her daily purchases, while Fred is learning to manage a fixed income using assets from the sale of the house that his kids grew up in, and Sam might need to be educated as to different investment strategies related to his 401(k) account.

When we think about *purpose*, this can range from concrete examples to the philosophical. Purpose to an individual can mean how they view the value of their job or profession. The COVID-19 crisis caused a lot of professional people to reflect on the importance (or nonimportance) of their job as they coped with physical dislocation from their offices and colleagues, while others were literally on the front lines of a daily battle pondering if they were properly valued. Purpose can be cultural, such as how an individual views the standing of their position in their family as a breadwinner or a stay-at-home parent. Purpose can tie to religion and philosophy, causing us to consider what it is we hope to accomplish while we are living on this planet. How do we get the right experiences? How do we avoid what today has become known as FOMO (fear of missing out)?

My intent here, as it has been in all my frameworks, is not to exhaust all of these lists. Rather, it might help you quickly think about the assembly of resources that might be arrayed, displayed, or set in front of a specific person (consumer). Such a list might be vast but is kind of fun to think about if you like organizing things. Just like when you go to your grocery store or to the local hardware store with our expert, somebody has gone to the effort to think about how to label the aisles, what needs to be in inventory, how to price it, and, if they are really good, how it all fits together to complete a project. Before entering these venues, you make a list of the things you need, a "shopping list," to ensure you are solving your problem at hand. In the broader case of this book, we think of the problem to be the achievement of total health and well-being for a consumer. I trust you can see that the leadership of any incumbent healthcare organizations or innovative point solutions should be pressing the question "How do I make sure I have the right inventory of health resources available in the right categories (aisles) at the right price so that the input cost of using these resources results in higher health status and higher total well-being than if we only rely on the traditional clinical healthcare professionals?"

When Clinical Care and Daily Living Are Brought Together

Information technology applied properly can bring scale to big and important ideas. Information technology that understands a person within a set of objectives—in this case, getting the right set of inputs for daily living to complement the inputs of clinical care—can utilize this scale. This is true because the information technology in the systematic framework I've laid out uses big data and complex software to become very personal and meaningful for an individual. The illustration on the following page shows what we are systematically seeking to accomplish.

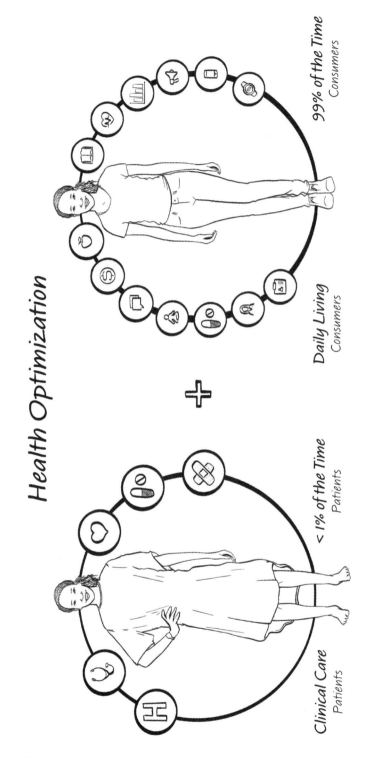

Health Optimization

99% of the Time
Consumers

Daily Living
Consumers

< 1% of the Time
Patients

Clinical Care
Patients

It's a simple picture, but a great deal of change must occur for the transformation from sickcare to health optimization to take place. One requirement of this vision is creating productive partnerships between the outstanding professionals serving the healthcare system, from clinicians and researchers to plan providers and government bureaucrats, with the kinds of resources that can address and integrate the needs of daily living. Forming such partnerships means taking highly innovative approaches to problem solving, which is why it takes all the aspects discussed in this book to address solutions to the current healthcare conundrum. My vision of optimized health for all will ask for more inquisitive thinking from all the stakeholders that occupy the clinical care portion of our equation's denominator because it inherently treats each individual's health in a more comprehensive way. Healthcare professionals will have to grow in their abilities to direct care using a broader slate of curated resources, including signals and data that haven't yet been taught in clinical curriculums. This doesn't have to be burdensome for those stakeholders. Quite the opposite. What I have proposed in developing a systematic framework will provide clinical care practitioners and others new tools to be better at what they already do best. They will have an ability to use the rich data we can provide them to better understand individual consumer needs. But to do so, they will have to be willing to let nonclinical ecosystem players sit at the "healthcare table."

It's likely you are familiar with CVS's acquisition of Aetna, which combined a leading retail pharmacy company with a large national health plan. For sure you are familiar with Walmart. No doubt the thoughtful executives who run these big corporations are working to find ways to transform beyond sickcare across the massive populations they serve—although there is a lot of money and profit in sickcare. But let's think smaller and more localized, and examine one incumbent nearly every person has experienced: the retail pharmacy. How are we dependent on them today, and what are the opportunities and pitfalls to think about related to how they could impact our health? Think for a moment: What community could survive without a pharmacy? The traditional pharmacy as it has evolved today is a handy representative example of so much we have been discussing in this book.

Picture whatever one you are already familiar with, whether that's a large chain we could all name or your local neighborhood mom-and-pop variety. They are a staple in the retail environment. Their absence is usually symbolic of a harbinger of death for a community's economic viability (as is the absence of a hardware store). Visit any town where the primary source of jobs has disappeared or a city where a once populous inner-city neighborhood has given way to redevelopment—as people begin to flee to find work or housing elsewhere, those who remain behind are put in even greater hardship once the community can no longer support a local pharmacy.

Now, when do you absolutely need a pharmacy? Obviously the answer is "When I need a prescription filled." Equally obviously, the script you need filled was written by another member of the clinical care community—your doctor or dentist or physician's assistant—which is a reminder of the interactivity of the various incumbents in the healthcare system. Perhaps you have a relationship with your pharmacist and have found that they are quite willing to answer questions and provide expertise on the products they dispense. In fact, they may be a lot like our imagined hardware store owner: full of helpful advice, knowledgeable about the products they sell, up to date on new medical findings regarding the use of prescription medicine, proactive in checking for drug interactions, capable of deciphering some of what your doctor has told you in language you can understand.

Your pharmacist is an expert in their discipline in a field that is demanding and competitive. But he or she is also a retailer, or at least affiliated with one. To that end—following the same essential principles used in the design of a casino's layout—in order to reach the pharmacy counter you will have passed through aisle upon aisle of over-the-counter medical products, a vast array of beauty products and household items, likely all the merchandise you associate with a convenience store, and several aisles of food. Just as likely, if your pharmacy is located in one corner of your grocery store, reaching it takes you past an array of other things to purchase.

Okay, so you're saying, "This is familiar; what's your point?" Well, there are several, actually. On the face of it, you already see in a retail environment how intertwined these products of healthcare—pharmaceuticals and medical supply products—are with products we associate with daily living—food, beer, sunglasses, diapers (of the infant and the adult varieties), lots and lots of candy and soft drinks. A first and central point: There's already retail integration of the various items in our equation denominator even when there is little formal integration in how "healthcare" regards "health." A second point: If your only use of a pharmacy were for prescribed medications, how often would you set foot in the store? Once a month, if you have regular prescriptions? Once or twice a year, if you don't? That's a pretty direct reinforcement of how little time we spend in the immediate presence of clinical settings (even, relatively speaking, for the "sickest" among us). And a third point: As you walk down that long candy aisle or past the one overflowing with chips and snacks or beyond the coolers filled with sugary, caffeinated soft drinks, is it too much of a stretch to think that what we eat should have as much of an effect on our health as the pills we are picking up in the back of the store? Shouldn't how often we imbibe alcohol or what we do for recreation also be factors?

Isn't that common sense? A fourth point: We are entirely familiar with a consumer-driven economy in which we are constantly being sold things we not only don't need but whose consumption may also have a directly negative impact on our health. Your typical pharmacy is an embodiment of this reality. Despite the media headline callouts of multibillion-dollar big-pharma profits, most of these profits don't trickle down to the retail outlet. As a result, those pharmacies really need you to buy your batteries, shampoo, or perfume, and grab a snack, as you pass through. The irony can be palpable, for when Sarah goes to pick up her insulin, she's met with a deluge of snack foods she shouldn't consume if she is to control her diabetes.

Of course, the bigger point is that pharmacies aren't the only examples of such irony. The doctor who tells you that a lot of your health issues would be alleviated if you lost weight and were more active may very well be overweight. Medscape's 2014 "Physician Lifestyle Report" found that 34 percent of physicians were overweight, on par with the 35 percent national average for the larger population, and 8 percent of doctors self-identified as obese. More than 40 percent of them reported eating a diet high in meat, fat, and carbs.[35] Such behavior exemplifies the divide between sound health practice and actual life behavior. Such ironies are common and can bring a smile as you contemplate how the massive profits derived from treating impotency fueled by some eyebrow-raising commercials in turn help to generate research funding for lifesaving medications. And some ironies can also be unintentionally horrific, such as how physicians' humane desire to alleviate pain and suffering in their patients have helped fuel addiction to prescription opioid painkillers. We see hospital stays shortened because hospital visits *increase* the risk of acquiring hard-to-treat bacterial infections. We see product manufacturers shape and size candies nearly identically to drug pills and flavor vaping potions and create varying devices that mimic the "dangerous" use of tobacco and inhalation of illegal substances. Such ironies abound. What do they show us? Quite simply, nearly every aspect of our daily living has intended and unintended health consequences.

The best way to avoid unintended consequences, in my experience, is to be intentional. This chapter has helped us gain an understanding of what it takes to create an intelligent ecosystem, for both clinical care and daily living, that

Quite simply, nearly every aspect of our daily living has intended and unintended health consequences.

will intentionally support a person or a population to achieve their highest health status and total well-being. Going back to chapter 5, it helps further explain the expanded view of what we need to consider in defining the consumer wallet in healthcare. And we'd better understand that it's not just about putting the components in place but also creating a system where health improvement resources are partnered and integrated into daily living on a timely basis with sponsorship from the traditional healthcare incumbents in an evolved type of benefit plan. Ultimately, productive partnerships are like a successful marriage—not only is the one partner present for the support of the other, but the knowledge base is also expanded while the workload is divided.

MOVING FROM SICKCARE TO HEALTH OPTIMIZATION

Why would anybody need to write a book about something nearly everybody agrees on? The answer, simply, is that just because everybody agrees on a principle doesn't mean they know how to accomplish it. We would all appreciate safe nuclear cold fusion to produce power, but nobody has cracked the code yet. Moving from hard science to social constructs, nearly everybody can agree that reducing economic and social inequalities and racism is a desirable outcome, but thus far no entity or person has managed to sustainably orchestrate all the moving parts.

Let me affirmatively state that we have the ability to move our nation and the world from one of reactive sickcare to proactive health optimization. Further, let me be clear that this will produce an overall higher health status and total well-being across any population at a lower total cost than what is happening today. This systematic process is rooted in using a combination of clinical and daily living data to personalize and localize resources for individuals that are specifically targeted to improve their health and total well-being. In this case, what's good for one person is also good for all people. And, through the use of information technology that need not be invented—but rather integrated and applied—health optimization can be scaled to not just the hundreds of millions of people in the United States but also to billions of people around the world.

I have yet to meet a leader in any incumbent healthcare entity that doesn't philosophically and morally agree with the idea that the strengths of the traditional healthcare system can be combined with innovation in analytics and consumer interactions to produce much better health at much greater efficiency. The same is true of leaders of all types of business and government institutions. So what is the rub?

I said at the outset of this book that past efforts to create major breakthroughs in advancing the value of a healthcare system have consistently excluded the most important actor in the equation— the consumer. This is because the healthcare system as it has existed has primarily focused on doing things to patients. And again, while improving capabilities and quality in patient care is a great thing, it's not enough of a thing to transform the healthcare system. We must take a more holistic view of a person not just in words—which is easy—but in systems and in actions. Building out scalable systems requires the codification of knowledge into process frameworks that require data and software technology to achieve. This book has been an extended how-to examination for solving the seemingly intractable problem of moving the healthcare system from focusing on sickcare, which it does pretty darn well, to advancing every consumer's journey toward optimal health.

By chance I was refining the content of this book during the outbreak of the COVID-19 pandemic and the uptick in awareness of embedded racism. There could not have been stronger logical proof of the fundamentals in this book. If you looked carefully at the horrific war with the COVID-19 virus, you saw how the rush to reactive sickcare sucked all the oxygen out of the room, no pun intended. As normal preventive and routine clinical care was set aside, or delayed (temporarily, I hope), the overall health status of our nation was lowered far more than the direct impact of COVID-19 itself. It also highlighted how many organizations and people were able to quickly adapt to use virtual technology to connect to resources that could support aspects of daily living, like nutrition and fitness, and use telemedicine and telemonitoring to virtually access clinical care. Even prior to incidents that thrust racism to the forefront of daily conversations, COVID-19 statistics led the media to put a spotlight on the vulnerability of disadvantaged minority populations as it relates to health status. The subsequent rising tide of protests appropriately led to "pledges" of actions, which sounded good. But I must share with you that I believe most good intentions are hollow if you don't have a way to precisely identify who needs what kind of specific resources in a personalized and localized way and get those resources connected to them within an economic framework that is sustainable. The frameworks in this book, because they address health and total well-being and apply social determinants, will help us untangle these difficult challenges.

A Quick Review of the Path to Health Optimization

Health optimization is something that can always be improved. In healthcare, higher value is achieved when the input costs to achieve and maintain a higher health status are lower relative to the status achieved. The two major input

In healthcare, higher value is achieved when the input costs to achieve and maintain a higher health status are lower relative to the status achieved.

categories are clinical care and daily living, and these both are highly impacted by the big data science of "omics" and social determinants of health (SDoH), respectively. This gives us our unifying equation for creating higher healthcare value through the pursuit of health optimization.

$$H_v = \frac{\textit{Health Status (person or population)}}{\textit{Clinical Care ("omics") + Daily Living (SDoH)}}$$

We keep the following principles in mind as we execute on this equation:

1. People are sometimes patients but always consumers.

2. The type of benefit plan a person has "sets the table" for the denominator.

3. We must understand the year-in-the-life of the consumer to understand the problem(s) they are trying to solve.

4. Healthcare incumbent entities, no matter their type, have eight common reasons (the eight stripes) they need to engage with consumers, and these reasons support the consumers as well.

5. There are numerous point solutions in the market that can support a consumer in daily living, as well as clinically.

6. Consumers have only a few related incumbent healthcare entities, but there are many point solutions. These must be brought together systematically.

7. A categorized, personalized, localized arrangement of clinical and daily living health improvement resources curated by healthcare incumbent organizations becomes an intelligent ecosystem surrounding consumers.

8. Data science that combines clinical and daily living, when applied through codified information technology that reflects the knowledge of experts, is both possible and required, and data privacy matters are manageable.

9. Health optimization encompasses both the achievement and maintenance of a person's highest health status and supports the holistic attainment of total well-being.

What Systematic Health Optimization Could Look Like

As we contemplate the pursuit of health optimization, let's take a look at what this approach can yield for our four consumers. Let's reimagine what Fred's, María's, Sarah's, and Sam's lives might look like if the principles in this book were applied.

Fred

Fred isn't addicted to technology in the way that Sam is, but he's long been adept at using his desktop computer, and he's found himself trying several of the suggestions he's found in his daily health news email feed provided through his Medicare Advantage health plan. He first tried a seminar called "Financial Planning in Your Seventies." That felt comfortable to Fred because he'd overseen numerous accounts in his days as a salesman and had dallied in investments. He learned how to create more income yield out of the proceeds from the sale of his house without putting his children's inheritance at risk. He met a couple of new faces in the seminar who were in the similar position of caring for spouses struggling with dementia, and he talked with them about a support group he'd been sent information about. The three decided to try the group together, and Fred was surprised to learn how easy it was to chat with others in his same predicament. He received good suggestions for how best to help his wife, and he enjoyed telling his wife about new people he'd met in the group.

At his most recent doctor's appointment, which he scheduled online, he was given the number to a hotline he could call with questions about his wife's care that put him in direct contact with a nurse. During a visit for himself, Fred and his doctor were able to review all of his medications right on the doctor's tablet computer. At the end of the appointment, his doctor told him how much he wanted Fred to work on improving his balance and told him that he'd have his office staff send him some suggestions through his health optimization platform, which were part of his health benefits plan. One of those suggestions was a weekly class titled "Tai Chi for Balance." At first Fred thought it was going to be some hippy-dippy thing, but he'd mentioned it to a favorite staff waitress at dinner, and she'd encouraged him to go. He gave it a try and met several people he enjoyed. After attending regularly for two months and even practicing some at home, he felt more relaxed and more stable on his feet. He feels more confident in his ability to help provide his wife much of her daily care, and that makes him feel good about himself. He's made some new friends in the past couple months and found someone he trusts to stay with his wife twice a week while he plays cards with these friends. He feels reaffirmed in his ability to help his wife.

María

María, because she received a fitness program credit on her health optimization platform from her employer, gave yoga a try for the first time. Her doctor had renewed warnings that her A1C had placed her in a prediabetic condition and emphasized that proper diet and exercise could stabilize her blood sugar. Yoga seemed a manageable starting point. There she met a group of women she enjoyed and with whom she had a lot in common. She joined several of them for a step class at a gym near her office and found it reminded her of dancing, something she loved when she was younger. She was doubly pleased to learn that her employee benefits plan included a fifty-fifty match on a gym membership. She's become such a regular at the gym that she often goes for coffee with her new friends. One of them is a financial planner. María has begun to talk with her about money worries. This financial counselor has helped her see that she has equity in her home and that it's okay if she and her husband borrow against that equity to see them through other financial objectives. She's learned how to put their net worth to work for them, so she doesn't feel like she's on a precarious financial treadmill.

Feeling better physically and with newfound peace of mind, she even has convinced her mother to attend a gentle flow yoga class with her. They catch up on the drive to class and talk about her mother's health concerns and family issues. As the pounds have come off, María feels rejuvenated, cooks healthier foods at home more often, and has even gotten her husband to start thinking more about how he eats. Her husband even accessed one of the point solution programs available on her employer's health optimization platform to understand how to manage his stress and avoid overuse of alcohol. Last week her husband surprised her by taking her dancing.

Sarah

When the clinic near Sarah's apartment told her about a free health optimization app she could use that would help her control numerous aspects of her own healthcare right from her phone, she was curious. Her phone often felt like her lifeline anyway. Once she opened the app, she couldn't believe what she found: Not only could she book her clinic appointments and upload her blood sugar monitor results, but there was also a huge list of resources that had been built specifically for her needs. She found a link to a babysitting app that had vetted all the recommended providers in her neighborhood. She received news of a child support group for kids with asthma, as well as a class for kids managing asthma put on by a respiratory specialist who practiced at her local clinic. And she was shocked to discover that there was a truck selling fresh fruit and vegetables that set up only ten blocks from her apartment, and she even received discount coupons that saved her 30 percent as long as she recorded the purchase. She'd always wanted to incorporate more fresh food in her family's meals, but she never felt she could afford it, and trying to get to a grocery store with decent produce required two transfers and the hassle of lugging groceries on crowded buses. Her girls' eyes lit up the first time they tasted really fresh avocados. One of the workers on the produce truck showed her how she could have their blog linked right to the app; it was full of menu ideas and recipes and even talked about cooking demonstrations they sponsored at a community center where her kids went to after-school programs.

One night at the community center, she reconnected with a cousin who was just a year younger than Sarah and also a single mom. Sarah was impressed with how well her cousin had her life together, holding down a good job. Her cousin seemed so happy and stable. They soon rekindled a friendship—they had been close as adolescents—and soon they started to turn to one another to look after one another's kids. With somewhere safe for her daughters to be several evenings a week, she acted on her cousin's encouragement and signed up for a two-week class at the community college. That experience gave her the courage to sign up for an Excel course. Not only did she discover she had real skill at developing spreadsheets, but there was a state program that would help offset the cost of the course. Maybe best of all was the emotion she felt when she overheard her seven-year-old daughter tell a friend, "My mommy's really smart; she's going to college and getting all As." With her improved health and improved outlook on life, Sarah has recently begun to date a nice guy she met on campus.

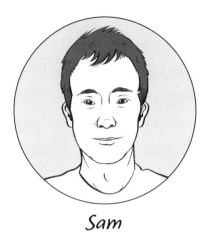

Sam

Sam recently hurt his knee playing volleyball at a company picnic. It wasn't serious, requiring nothing more than a visit to an urgent care facility. Mostly it was embarrassing to get hurt in front of coworkers, particularly several attractive women his age. He had a hard time admitting it to himself, but he'd fallen because he'd had a couple too many beers and, because he's not in the best of shape, didn't have the physical dexterity to arrest his fall. He'd been reluctant to go to the picnic at all because he often felt awkward around people in social settings. It was so much easier just to stay home, order some food off Grubhub, and play video games. But that was feeling pretty lonely lately. The picnic was kind of a wake-up call that his thirties were going to be different, physically at least, from his twenties. Besides, some of the unattached ladies there seemed genuinely nice when they talked to him. He thought he'd heard some of them talking about a climbing gym they wanted to try, and when he found a link to it in a health optimization app that his employer provided that allowed him to apply some incentive dollars, he decided to give it a try. He discovered that there were a number of other "singles" who, like him, were new to climbing. He was surprised to learn that he liked the challenge climbing provided, and he enjoyed the pride of completing a route and the comradery of being part of a group. He quickly realized that excessive drinking was good for neither his fitness nor his balance. The experience gave him enough confidence in the health optimization platform that he tried several other of its recommendations. He's looking forward to a scheduled climbing/camping trip he planned with several people he met at the gym. And he is looking forward to the next company event, where he might show off his newfound confidence alongside his smaller waist. For the first time, he sees the benefits of good habits, and he has begun to believe he could be a participant in a healthy relationship.

Just as one social determinant can start a domino effect that can cause substantial health problems and poor life consequences, the right action on another social determinant can put someone on a path to realizing better health and total well-being—access to the right resources at the right time can be truly transformative. What is the ultimate aim of a health system if not to help people be healthy—indeed, as healthy as every individual is capable of being? Until we solidify our focus on this ultimate outcome, we really won't solve the problems of access or affordability. In the spirit of the wedding vow from which I take this book's title, we must learn again "to love and to cherish" every individual the healthcare system serves, which of course means learning to cherish each person's right to live their best life. And it means we must cherish and nurture our own health such that we each become our own best advocates. I have real faith that the majority of people would seize this opportunity if provided a holistic platform with which to organize resources and take action. We owe it to each other to create the means to do so.

Now What?

That depends!

If you read this book from the perspective of a consumer who is living your daily life and is interested in healthcare, you are now in a position to discern how your employer, health plan, clinicians, pharmacy, and local organizations can help assist you through your year-in-the-life, and you can seek the right types of personalized and localized resources to solve the problems you want to solve.

If you are a worker in some aspect of healthcare, in addition to becoming a healthier consumer, you are now better positioned to think about how your role in healthcare plays into a holistic set of clinical and daily living activities so that you can increase your sensitivity to siloed behaviors and be of the best help to the person—whether they are a patient, employee, member, or consumer at that moment—in the context of your job.

If you are a healthcare industry leader, influencer, information technologist, or investor, you now have a set of frameworks and a unifying equation that you can choose to pursue, improve, or rip apart for its flaws. Perhaps all three. In any and all cases, our industry and all people served by it will be better off if you give serious thought to the "how" of what we all agree on. We must move from a reactive healthcare system to a proactive, holistic one that respects and is integrated with the clinical world but also transcends it.

I understand that just deciphering the sickcare system of doctors, specialists, pharmacies, emergency rooms, urgent care centers, and hospitals is tough. I get it. But remember that the whole of clinical care accounts for 30 percent of our total health. Tougher still is navigating the world of daily living and resources that impact 70 percent of our health day in, day out within our social determinants and with the knowledge to pivot off your benefit plan. Yet don't we all deserve a holistic system that supports us at any point in our year-in-the-life? I hope this book has shown what a systematic approach to the problem can look like, has shown respect for the tradition of the way healthcare operates today, and has shown a realistic path toward achieving and sustaining optimal health for every person while improving the underlying cost and affordability of healthcare.

To health optimization!

ACKNOWLEDGMENTS

No individual person can accomplish meaningful pursuits without the help of others. Neither is it possible for me to list all of those who, throughout my life and career, have supported me, endured me, and pushed me to contribute the most I can to improve the world in which we live. While my last book, *The Healthcare Cure* (Prometheus, 2011), deconstructed the still-existing world of the US healthcare system in an effort to encourage the use of information technology for the integration of traditional benefits and care, *Not Just in Sickness … But Also in Health* is much farther reaching. The pursuit of health optimization to transform our healthcare system is a goal that I share with many like-minded industry colleagues. I truly appreciate the efforts of all those who drive excellence and breakthroughs in our current clinical system and those who are seeking to innovate with deep respect for what we know and do today while transcending to the next level of improving health with greater holistic systematic thinking, methods, and technologies.

The logistics of producing substantive content on an innovative topic are daunting—especially in the form of a book. I want to thank all of my former colleagues at Welltok, and TriZetto before that, where I tested my thinking with real-life applied solutions that were never easy to accomplish but always fruitful. Most recently, the leaders at the organizations where I have served as a board member or advisor—including Alignment Healthcare, NextGen Healthcare, TriNetX, Hoag Health System, the UCI Center for Digital Transformation, and the Oliver-Wyman Health Innovation Center—allow me to immerse myself each and every day in different lenses across the healthcare spectrum. Frankly, it is impossible to stop learning and challenging myself to do better when I have the privilege to interact with such great people

On a practical level, *Not Just in Sickness ... But Also in Health* required some serious heavy lifting to assemble. Thank you to Mark Leichliter, who worked with me to distill complex concepts into consumable prose. He, along with the talented Advantage team at Forbes, was enduring and patient. Also, my thanks to Erica Morgenstern, Welltok's chief communications officer, who initially helped organize my content and was an insistent and supportive voice that I get this book completed and published to move our industry forward.

I will share with you the irony that while I was writing this book about how to think beyond "sickcare," I experienced a number of serious health issues. These were the most significant and perplexing medical challenges for me and my doctors since my seven Crohn's disease–related major surgeries from 1990 to 1995, where I spent nearly a hundred days as an inpatient. I also became a grandfather and continued to be blessed by the support of my wife, my daughters, and their husbands. The experience only underscored that you must have both excellent clinical care and complementary daily living support to achieve and maintain your highest health status.

To health optimization!

SOURCES

1   Hood, Gennuso, Swain, and Catlin, "County Health Rankings: Relationships between Determinant Factors and Health Outcomes," *American Journal of Preventive Medicine* 50, no. 2, 2016: 129–135.

2   Bradley Sawyer and Gary Claxton, "How Do Health Expenditures Vary Across the Population?" Peterson-KFF Health System Tracker, January 16, 2019. www.healthsystemtracker.org/chart-collection/health-expenditures-vary-across-population/#item-start.

3   Henry J. Kaiser Family Foundation, "Health Insurance Coverage of the Total Population." https://www.kff.org/other/state-indicator/total-population/?currentTimeframe=0&sortModel=%7B%22colId%22:%22Location%22,%22sort%22:%22asc%22%7D.

4   Henry J. Kaiser Family Foundation. "2018 Employer Health Benefits Survey." www.kff.org/health-costs/ eport/2018-employer-health-benefits-survey/.

5   National Business Group on Health, "Best Employers—Excellence in Health and Well-Being." http://www.wbgh.org/best-employers/.

6   Henry J. Kaiser Family Foundation. "Health Insurance Coverage of Children 0–18." https://www.kff.org/other/state-indicator/children-0-18/?currentTimeframe=0&sortModel=%7B%22colId%22:%22Location%22,%22sort%22:%22asc%22%7D.

7   Henry J. Kaiser Family Foundation. "Where Are States Today? Medicaid and CHIP Eligibility Levels for Children, Pregnant Women, and Adults." https://www.kff.org/medicaid/fact-sheet/where-are-states-today-medicaid-and-chip/.

8   Michele Ver Ploeg, "Access to Affordable, Nutritious Food Is Limited in 'Food Deserts,'" United States Department of Agriculture, Economic Research Service. https://www.ers.usda.gov/amber-waves/2010/march/access-to-affordable-nutritious-food-is-limited-in-food-deserts/.

9   Ver Ploeg.

10 Henry J. Kaiser Foundation, "Medicaid's Role in Financing Behavioral Health Services for Low-Income Individuals." https://www.kff.org/medicaid/issue-brief/medicaids-role-in-financing-behavioral-health-services-for-low-income-individuals/.

11 Henry J. Kaiser Foundation." Health Insurance Coverage of the Total Population." https://www.kff.org/other/state-indicator/total-population/?currentTimeframe=0&sortModel=percent7Bpercent22colIdpercent22:percent22Locationpercent22,percent22sortpercent22:percent22asc percent22percent7D.

12 Juliette Cubanski, Tricia Neuman, and Meredith Freed, "The Facts on Medicare Spending and Financing," August 20, 2019. https://www.kff.org/medicare/issue-brief/the-facts-on-medicare-spending-and-financing/.

13 Kim Parker, Rich Morin, and Juliana Menasce Horowitz, "3 Views of Demographic Change," Pew Research Center. https://www.pewsocialtrends.org/2019/03/21/views-of-demographic-changes-in-america/.

14 Megan Multack and Claire Noel-Miller, "Who Relies on Medicare? Profile of the Medicare Population," AARP Public Policy Institute.www.aarp.org/content/dam/aarp/research/public_policy_institute/health/who-relies-on-medicare-factsheet-AARP-ppi-health.pdf.

15 Veterans Administration, "VA Benefits & Health Care Utilization." https://www.va.gov/vetdata/docs/pocketcards/fy2019q3.PDF.

16 Health.mil, "Beneficiary Population Statistics." https://www.health.mil/I-Am-A/Media/Media-Center/Patient-Population-Statistics.

17 Ezra Dyer, "How Kia Got Good," Popular Mechanics online, January 4, 2018. /www.popularmechanics.com/cars/car-technology/a14416136/how-kia-got-good/.

18 Andis Robeznieks, "Social Determinants of Health: What They Are, What They Aren't," American Medical Association, Patient Support and Advocacy, February 3, 2020. https://www.ama-assn.org/delivering-care/patient-support-advocacy/social-determinants-health-what-they-are-what-they-arent.

19 Anna Bahney, "40 Percent of Americans Can't Cover a $400 Emergency Expense," CNN Money, May 22, 2018. https://money.cnn.com/2018/05/22/pf/emergency-expenses-household-finances/index.html.

20 Markian Hawryluk, "Nothing to Sneeze At: $2,659 Bill to Pluck Doll's Shoe From Girl's Nose," NPR Illinois, November 26, 2019. https://www.nprillinois.org/post/nothing-sneeze-2659-bill-pluck-dolls-shoe-girls-nose#stream/0.

21 Linda Carroll, "Can Alzheimer's Be Stopped? Five Lifestyle Behaviors Are Key, New Research Suggests," NBC News, https://www.nbcnews.com/health/can-alzheimer-s-be-stopped-five-lifestyle-behaviors-are-=key-n1029441.

22 Centers for Medicare and Medicaid Services, "NHE Fact Sheet." https://www.cms.gov/research-statistics-data-and-systems/statistics-trends-and-reports/nationalhealthexpenddata/nhe-fact-sheet.

23 CDC, "STEADI (Stopping Elderly Accidents, Deaths, and Injuries) Initiative." https://www.cdc.gov/steadi/about.html.

24   Lucia Torres, "Simple Ways to Prevent Falls in Older Adults," NPR
     Weekend Edition Sunday, July 14, 2019. https://www.npr.org/sections/
     health-shots/2019/07/14/741310765/simple-ways-to-prevent-falls-in-
     older-adults?utm_source=npr_newsletter&utm_medium=email&utm_
     content=20190715&utm_campaign=npr_email_a_friend&utm_
     term=storyshare.

25   Pew, "Mobile Phone Ownership Over Time." https://www.pewinternet.
     org/fact-sheet/mobile/.

26   Centers for Medicare and Medicaid Services, "Centers for Medicare &
     Medicaid Services." https://www.cms.gov/Research-Statistics-Data-and-
     Systems/Statistics-Trends-and-Reports/NationalHealthExpendData/Nat
     ionalHealthAccountsHistorical#:~:text=U.S.%20health%20care%20
     spending%20grew,spending%20accounted%20for%2017.7%20percent.

27   Donald M. Berwick, Thomas W. Nolan, and John Whittington, "The
     Triple Aim: Care, Health, And Cost," Health Affairs (May/June 2008).
     https://www.healthaffairs.org/doi/full/10.1377/hlthaff.27.3.759.

28   National Conference of State Legislatures, "Health Insurance: Premiums
     and Increases," December 4, 2018. http://www.ncsl.org/research/health/
     health-insurance-premiums.aspx.

29   National Conference of State Legislatures.

30   National Council on Disability, "An Overview of Medicaid Managed
     Care." https://www.ncd.gov/policy/chapter-1-overview-medicaid-man-
     aged-care.

31   Bradley Sawyer and Cynthia Cox, "How does health spending in the
     U.S. compare to other countries?" Health System Tracker, December
     7, 2018. https://www.healthsystemtracker.org/chart-collection/
     health-spending-u-s-compare-countries/#item-start.

32 Esteban Ortiz-Ospina and Max Roser, "Government spending," Our World in Data, https://ourworldindata.org/government-spending.

33 US Bureau of Labor Statistics, "Economic Situation Summary," June 5, 2020. https://www.bls.gov/news.release/empsit.nr0.htm.

34 IBM, "IBM's Culture of Health," https://www.ibm.com/ibm/responsibility/employee_well_being.shtml.

35 Molly Gamble, "How Healthy Are Physicians?" Becker's Hospital Review, January 24, 2014. https://www.beckershospitalreview.com/hospital-physician-relationships/how-healthy-are-physicians.html.